STANIER
LOCOMOTIVE CLASSES

STANIER
LOCOMOTIVE CLASSES

A. J. POWELL

LONDON
IAN ALLAN LTD

First published 1991

ISBN 0 7110 1962 2

© Ian Allan Ltd 1991

Published by Ian Allan Ltd, Shepperton, Surrey;
and printed by Ian Allan Printing Ltd at their works
at Coombelands in Runnymede, England

Below:
No 46205 *Princess Victoria* **(Crewe, 7/35) seen
within the confines of Crewe North MPD. The
massive motion bracket was the result of a
1938 modification to the inside valve gear.**
J. R. Carter

Below right:
**No 48348 (Horwich, 04/44) amongst other
Stanier locomotives at Rose Grove MPD on the
last day of normal steam working, 3 August
1968.** *J. H. Bird*

Contents

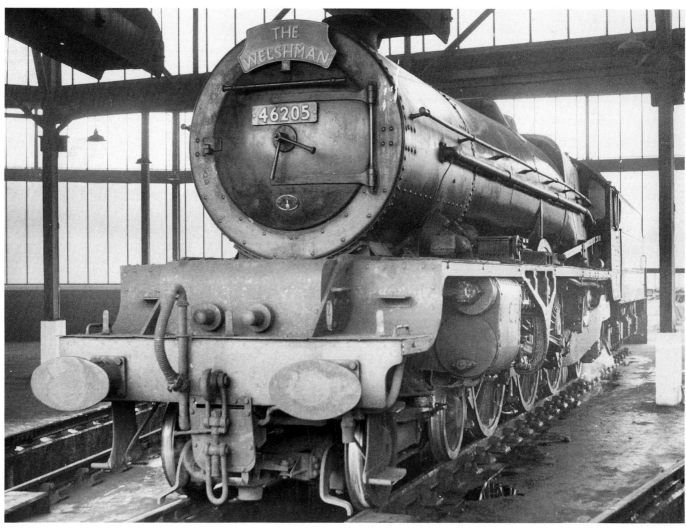

Preface

Recognition of Stanier locomotives? 'Anyone with the slightest knowledge of steam locomotives can recognise one', I hear you say. Even against a background of Egyptian palm trees or Turkish mosques they stand out unmistakably. Why a book on the subject? There is more to it than that, of course. Gaze at the preserved No 6201 *Princess Elizabeth* and study a picture of the next in series, No 46202 *Princess Anne;* why do they appear significantly different? How is it that No 6170 *British Legion* in prewar LMSR crimson lake looked different from the same locomotive years later in BR Brunswick green? And why did both look different from the previous in series No 46169, even in the same livery? Why do similar tenders or side tanks exhibit different rivet patterns – or no rivets at all? And if you are modelling a particular Class 5 4-6-0, which of three types of chimney do you put on it?

This book attempts to cover the visual features of each class and how they changed over the years, either in the course of construction or during their years of service. It is an attempt fraught with difficulty and many pitfalls after a lapse of 25 years and more, and the indecent haste with which steam – and many of the records relating to it – were eradicated during the 1960s. Many hundreds of photographs have been studied for evidence of change to back up personal experience, fading recollection and records, but it still inevitably leaves loose ends.

I am indebted to two sources of factual data covering orders, construction, modifications and withdrawal. Peter Rowledge's *LMS Engines, Names, Numbers, Types and Classes* (David & Charles, 1989) is a mine of information, and the more recent *LMS Locomotive Design and Construction* by Arthur Cook and published by the RCTS is most valuable in opening up much hitherto unpublished material. I have dredged Ian Allan's large photographic library for pictures to illustrate specific variations within locomotive classes. I am grateful to Pat Whitehouse of Millbrook House Ltd for permission to use a number of the splendid pictures by the late Bishop Eric Treacy. Jim Jarvis and Phil Lynch have been most helpful in giving me a selection of their photographs, which illustrate particular points of design and in the process have corrected some misconceptions.

The overall result will certainly not be the last word on a fascinating subject. Nevertheless, I hope that I have brought together factual information and photographic evidence from a multiplicity of separate sources into a useful single volume, which will add to the sum of knowledge for steam locomotive enthusiasts and serious modellers alike.

A. J. Powell
Winterley
Nr Sandbach
Cheshire

Introduction

In the 1930s two Chief Mechanical Engineers of railways in Britain dominated the steam locomotive engineering world. One was H. N. (later Sir Nigel) Gresley of the LNER; the other — and arguably the greater of the two — was William Arthur Stanier. He revolutionised the locomotive stock of the LMSR, in terms both of performance and of mechanical excellence, and laid a firm foundation on which two subsequent LMSR CMEs, C. E. Fairburn and H. G. Ivatt, and the Member for Mechanical Engineering at the nationalised Railway Executive, R. A. Riddles, were proud to apply newer developments. He was a giant in his field.

Nothing less than a giant was needed. As the 1930s opened, the locomotive side of the LMSR was in deep trouble. Formed in 1923 as an amalgamation of two major railways, the Midland and the LNWR/L&YR, which had provided their locomotives and operated their trains in two radically opposed traditions, together with several smaller but no less important railways including the far-flung Scottish companies, the new organisation required a strong hand in charge of its locomotive activities working in harmony with an enlightened operating department which knew what it wanted, both presently and in the next decade. In practice, it got neither.

The influence of the Midland Railway was deep-seated. The first CME, George Hughes from the Lancashire & Yorkshire Railway, was the senior man and expanded his headquarters at Horwich, but was to hold office for less than three years before retiring

prematurely in disillusion. He was not his own master, even in his own department; the *éminence grise* who in practice wielded the authority and exercised powers of veto was an ex-Derby chief draughtsman of strong will but narrow vision, James Anderson, who was now Superintendent of Motive Power within the operating department. His was the voice behind the annual building programmes, even if they bore the signatures of the Chief General Superintendent (the operating chief), the Chief Mechanical Engineer and the Chief Accountant. A dyed-in-the-wool Midland man, small locomotives, light trains, double heading *et al*, Anderson saw all the problems of the new company in the light, and soluble by the methods, of Midland philosophy. In this he was perhaps unwittingly abetted by the Chief Civil Engineer, who was having to work within bridge strength on the Midland Division which, while adequate for the Midland's 0-6-0s and 4-4-0s, imposed severe, in some cases insurmountable difficulties in designing large locomotives such as Hughes had in mind — Pacifics and 2-8-2s or 2-10-0s. So his lasting monument, which did not appear until after his departure, was a 2-6-0 mixed traffic locomotive, of thoroughly modern concept and detailing, whose design emanated from Horwich and largely survived determined attempts from Derby to 'Midlandise' it. The quite inappropriate tender was the most visible sign of this erosion. Ultimately no fewer than 245 of them were built. But otherwise the new builds during Hughes' short reign — apart from some leftovers from the

pre-Grouping companies — comprised Midland 4-4-0 compounds, Midland Class 4F 0-6-0s and Midland Class 3F 0-6-0Ts. The guiding hand behind this was not hard to seek.

With Hughes' retirement Henry Fowler, the deputy CME and previous CME of the Midland Railway, took over and moved the CME headquarters to Derby, now firmly established as the fount of all wisdom. In the other main drawing offices their familiar worlds were in total eclipse. Crewe, proud of the LNWR tradition (the 'Premier Line') and of its locomotives — cheap to build, generally well engineered if at times with dreadful lapses, and capable of out-performing anything from Derby — was largely ignored, left to sulk and lick its wounds, and tinker with its beloved 'Claughtons'. Horwich, after its moment of glory with the 2-6-0s, saw little new design work until Stanier's arrival; it attended to the modification of a 'Dreadnought' 4-6-0 as a four-cylinder compound (only to see the *raison d'être* for it disappear under Anderson's disapproval), the installation of poppet valve gear on five of the 2-6-0s built in 1929, and designed the little 0-6-0 dock tanks within strict Midland parameters, built at about the same time but nothing else of consequence. The St Rollox (ex-Caledonian Railway) office pottered about looking after the application of standard

Caledonian boilers to ex-Highland Railway locomotives, but was not involved in forward design thinking.

Fowler's prime interests lay not in the design of locomotives but in the workshops and in metallurgy. The Derby drawing office saw very little of him; design matters were left in the hands of his chief draughtsman, working to requirements agreed with Anderson. But locomotive policy was necessarily his concern, and even before Anderson admitted that Midland thinking would not operate the West Coast main line he could see the need for more powerful locomotives. The heavy Anglo-Scottish expresses needed bigger machines, and so did the heavy Toton-Brent coal flow. Anderson's panacea of 4-4-0 compounds was no match for Shap and Beattock; they had to work in pairs to handle the loads. Nor did the pre-Grouping designs match the needs. The LNWR 'Claughtons' were erratic in performance and very troublesome mechanically, while the L&YR 'Dreadnoughts' set to work between Crewe and Carlisle did not shine. In late 1925 preliminary design work started at Derby, with Crewe and Horwich participating as sub-contractors, on a pair of large four-cylinder compound locomotives, a 4-6-2 and a 2-8-2, using a common boiler and cylinders.

But a 4-6-2 was too big a leap from previous practice for Anderson to stomach and, ignoring Fowler, he persuaded top management that a new 4-6-0, comparable with the GWR's 'Castle' class, would meet all passenger requirements. Swindon loaned No 5000 Launceston Castle to the LMSR in September 1926 to show its capabilities between Euston and Carlisle. Impressed, management suggested buying 50 of the same, and when this proved impracticable, decided on a three-cylinder 4-6-0 and placed a 'design-and-build' contract with the North British Locomotive Co, Glasgow for 50 locomotives which became the 'Royal Scot' class. The need was desperate, with the operators planning a new 'Royal Scot' train service for the summer of 1927. Work on the new Pacific was killed.

The 2-8-2 proposal had also been undermined. Before his retirement Hughes had initiated discussions with Beyer, Peacock & Co in Manchester to explore whether a Beyer-Garratt articulated locomotive might prove capable of eliminating the double-heading on the Toton-Brent coal trains while meeting the Chief Civil Engineer's bridge limitations. From these discussions there soon crystallised a scheme for a 2-6-2+2-6-2 incorporating all the expertise of Beyer, Peacock gained in modern locomotive design for overseas. Simultaneously Anderson, unashamedly assuming the mantle of the CME, also started

Above:
The Stanier two-cylinder look. In the gloom of one of the roundhouses at Leeds Holbeck, Class 8F 2-8-0 No 48283 (North British, 8/42) undergoes piston valve repairs while Class 5 4-6-0 No 45138 (Armstrong Whitworth, 6/35) awaits its next duty. An early 1960s picture of grime and neglect.
Eric Treacy/Millbrook House collection

discussions with the firm on a parallel solution to the same problem, but in this case marking the cards to incorporate as much Midland practice as possible, with the coupled wheelbase and valve gear similar to that of the Derby-designed Somerset & Dorset Joint 2-8-0s, and widespread use of proportions from the Class 4F 0-6-0s of 1911 vintage. The resultant 2-6-0+0-6-2 for which Anderson, and not Fowler, signed the contract emerged in 1927 as (quite unnecessarily) an outdated design, potentially capable but a maintenance nightmare.

The same attitude also ruined the new 0-8-0 freight locomotives of 1929. The original LNWR Class G1, on which they were intended to be a major improvement, outlasted them. Only the Fowler 2-6-4Ts of 1927 matched the success of the 'Royal Scots' and the Hughes 2-6-0s, and in the all-important area of cylinder and valve gear design this was only due to a fortuitous and eleventh hour decision by Fowler himself which was completely out of character.

So when Sir Henry Fowler left the position of CME at the start of 1931, to be shunted sideways as Assistant to the Vice-President, he left behind a situation in which only 372 locomotives of modern concept had been built in the first eight years of the LMSR: 225 Hughes 2-6-0s, 70 'Royal

Scots', two 'Patriots' (nominally rebuilds) and 75 2-6-4Ts. There were another 157 which could have been reasonably satisfactory if only baleful Midland influences had been purged before birth. The remainder of the 9,319 steam locomotives in stock were of either pre-Grouping manufacture or design, getting long in the tooth — very much so in some cases — usually undersized for modern tasks, deteriorating in reliability and demanding increasing maintenance. In a word, the LMSR locomotive fleet was in crisis at a time when competition for traffic was becoming more acute with every month.

The appointment of Ernest J. H. Lemon as Fowler's successor was a holding operation and no more. He was essentially a carriage and wagon man, with limited knowledge of locomotive engineering. During his one-year occupancy the smouldering design feud between Midland and LNWR partisans intensified. The Derby and Crewe drawing offices came up with rival schemes to meet perceived requirements, with a measure of mutual contempt and very little common ground. It was no way to run a successful major railway.

Euston had recognised at this juncture that there was no in-house talent of sufficient stature to tackle this situation, knock heads together, get all pulling in the same direction and run a tight ship. The Vice-President responsible for engineering and research, Sir Harold Hartley, went head-hunting for a new man who would make a strong Chief Mechanical Engineer, unsullied by pre-Grouping rivalries, a sound locomotive engineer — the LMSR carriage and wagon function was in infinitely better shape than was the locomotive side — with a proven record. Late in 1931 Sir Harold found the man he was looking for; William Stanier was at the time Principal Assistant to the CME of the Great Western Railway at Swindon, then aged 56 and with wide experience of works management and locomotive running on that railway. On 1 January 1932 Stanier took up office at Euston.

His effective tenure was to last until the end of 1942, when he was seconded to the Government's Ministry of Production, though he kept in touch for another two years. During his 11 years he wrought a total revolution in the locomotive fleet of the LMSR, backed by the President, Sir Josiah Stamp, and supplied with Government money at low rates of interest to stimulate employment. The period was characterised firstly by deep economic depression — at this time new 4-6-0 locomotives could be bought for little over £6,000 apiece! — then of rearmament in the face of a rampant Nazi Germany, and finally of the difficult conditions of World War 2. He was responsible for putting into service 1,280 locomotives to his designs before his secondment, and thereafter several hundreds more were produced. It was a unique achievement on an enormous scale, which transformed the LMSR fleet from crisis to the very forefront of railway engineering.

There were three pressing needs when Stanier arrived at Euston. First was a large express passenger locomotive for the West Coast main line. The 'Royal Scots' handling the heaviest trains were doing magnificent work, but were limited to 420 tons north of Carnforth, and clearly management of the narrow firebox on the 401-mile Euston-Glasgow route was not consistent with through working, which the operators wanted. Also, competition was demanding increases in speed with progressively heavier loads, which they had not the capacity to deliver. Stanier's answer was the 1933 'Princess Royal' Pacifics, later developed into the magnificent 'Duchesses'.

The next need was for a more versatile mixed traffic engine, with a better turn of speed than the Hughes 2-6-0. This demanded larger coupled wheels and a leading bogie to provide smooth riding at speed, while keeping axleloads down to give the widest possible route availability. Using the GWR 'Hall' loosely as a prototype, Stanier produced the first Class 5 4-6-0 in 1934, a design so successful that it was steadily developed and built in large numbers for some 17 years, winning universal acclaim.

Finally an improved heavy general freight locomotive was called for. The existing 0-8-0s were acceptable for slow mineral traffic but a better speed range, more boiler power and easier preparation had to be provided for. The logical solution was a 2-8-0, which was introduced in 1935 and quickly took over the through freight workings; it was also sufficiently free-running to handle summer weekend passenger traffic when the demand for extra locomotives soared. It was also adopted by the Government early in World War 2 for overseas military service (though in the event the number so employed was relatively limited). The rest of his design work could be directed towards the modernisation and refinement of certain Fowler classes in accordance with his own engineering predilections.

Stanier brought with him a deeply held conviction of the rightness of many things emanating from Swindon. At the same time he was willing to recognise that some of its practices — the use of Stephenson valve gear between the frames on its modern two-cylinder locomotives, for instance — were not ideal and could be bettered. He was also big enough to accept that some of the more modern LMSR designs initiated during the Hughes and Fowler regimes, which had developed along lines differing from those of Swindon — the use of three cylinders where the GWR would have used four was a case in point — were worthy of further development rather than being tossed aside in favour of an alien approach. He was appreciative of the opinions of those who would drive and fire the locomotives he conceived. His was a 'hands on' approach, steering the work done both on the drawing board and on the shop floor, and seeking a feedback of information from the users. In this he was actively supported by a new chief draughtsman, the formidable Tom Coleman, with whom he established a real team relationship. He was not afraid to admit that some of his first ideas could be bettered; when this happened he would change course rapidly and without recrimination, if necessary leaving the relevant paperwork to catch up when it might. Stanier quickly earned recognition as a pillar of the British engineering establishment.

His locomotives were instantly recognisable, even against the unexpected backgrounds of Egyptian and Iranian deserts or Turkish mountains, where some finished their days. The tapered boiler with gently curved Belpaire firebox and top-feed fitting was a givaway; in all classes except the 'Duchess' the bottom of the boiler barrel was horizontal with all the taper on the top, making it clearly visible. So too was the rather severe-looking double side-window cab with its extended roof. Below the running board, the cylinders with their extended valve chests and pressure relief valves mounted on the covers, the twin slide-bars, the rather rangy Walschaerts valve gear laid out for long valve travel with its box-type expansion links and return cranks with four-stud fastening to the crank-pin ensured good efficiency. The wheels with their rigid triangular rims, built-up balance weights and (in the case of almost all tender classes) hollow axles were distinctive. Also for the tender locomotives the Stanier 4,000gal tender, its sides rolled in at the top over the edges of the bunker space, was an unmistakable trademark which has been emulated elsewhere. As soon as the driver reached for the whistle handle one's ears recognised a Stanier locomotive, even if it was out of sight a mile away — the deep note of the Caledonian hooter, often rather breathy (it always sounded more sure of itself when mounted vertically rather than horizontally) but always commanding respect. And the beat at the chimney; never as explosive as on a Swindon locomotive, never syncopated or muffled, but solid and at speed a veritable purr with every beat sharp and clear.

But style was less important than content. From the standpoints of enginemen, operators and running shed staff, the Stanier classes set new standards of performance, of comfort, of reliability, of thermal efficiency and of modest maintenance. They were characterised by sound engineering rather than adventurous bravado. Their boilers lasted the life of the locomotive. Until the shambles of neglect in the final years of steam, hot axleboxes were a rare event, something which only Swindon's locomotives could rival. They were fleet of foot, as witness the 114mph record of No 6220 Coronation in 1937; only the lack of a piece of railway comparable to the descent from Stoke Summit on the LNER's East Coast main line prevented this being pushed to 120mph or more. Men whistled as they worked them. And they lasted to the very end; steam on BR service trains finished when the fires were dropped from two Stanier Class 5s, Nos 45212 and 45318, on the night of 3 August 1968, and from Nos 45156 and 45318 on the following night after working special trains. It was fitting that three of Stanier's locomotives should have been in at the death.

Right:
The Stanier express passenger look. Kingmoor-based 'Jubilee' No 45724 Warspite (Crewe, 9/36) and 'Princess' No 46201 Princess Elizabeth (Crewe, 11/33) from Polmadie wait at the north end of Carlisle station to take over northbound expresses about 1961.
Eric Treacy/Millbrook House collection

General Notes

Locomotive Orders

From 1923 all locomotives built on LMSR account were produced against Lot Numbers, starting from 1 in that year and allocated progressively each year according to the types approved in the annual Building Programme. It was not normal practice to mark up the production drawings with these Lot Numbers until the formation of BR in 1948. Under LMSR practice the drawings showed the various Order Numbers allocated by the individual building works for accountancy purposes and (usually) the locomotive numbers corresponding to them, or in the case of outside contractor-built examples the firm's name and the locomotive numbers. From 1948 it became usual to show Lot Numbers and the corresponding locomotive numbers. This may help anyone consulting official drawings.

Renumbering

Apart from a handful of locomotives which changed or exchanged their numbers in special circumstances (see text) only one Stanier class was renumbered in LMSR days — the 40 2-6-0s built in 1933-34 (see page 28).

On the formation of British Railways in 1948, for a few months new and repaired locomotives were given an 'M' prefix to the normal number. This quickly gave way to the addition of 40,000 to the LMSR number. As a result it was necessary to manufacture and fit new smokebox door numberplates.

Locomotive Classification

The LMSR initially continued the general pre-Grouping practice of regarding locomotives as either passenger or freight. The concept of a mixed traffic locomotive had to await the coming of the Hughes 2-6-0s in 1926; thereafter it was very sparingly used, only two Stanier classes, ie the 2-6-0s (Nos 2945-2984) and the Class 5 4-6-0s (Nos 5000 onwards) being so regarded. These carried separate 'P' and 'F' classifications on the cab sides. The use of a single figure without suffix for mixed traffic locomotives was a BR development and followed reclassification to mixed traffic status of several previously passenger or freight classes.

Power Classification

The LMSR used a system of power classification for loading purposes, from 1 to 7 for passenger locomotives and 0 to 8 for freight and shunting locomotives. This classification was displayed on the cab side, in front of or just below the cab window(s). In the passenger group there was an additional class, 5X, introduced in 1930 for a new design of locomotive which was judged to fall midway between Classes 5 and 6; it was also carried by the Stanier 'Jubilee' 4-6-0s (see page 54).

In 1951 the system was adopted for all-line application, but the three top passenger classifications 5X, 6 and 7 were changed to 6, 7 and 8 respectively. No change was made to freight classifications, though the range was extended when the Class 9F 2-10-0s were built.

Liveries

To provide a complete and reliable account of livery changes to a particular class of locomotive, after the passage of so many years, is quite impossible; even to catalogue the general changes which took place can be both lengthy and riddled with exceptions. The LMSR went through several official changes — the 1936 liveries, reversion broadly to pre-1936, wartime plain black and the 1946 livery — all eroded by different

works practices and the using up of stocks of transfers. BR was also responsible for several livery developments (which are better documented). Accordingly this book confines itself to the general policy applications of the various liveries. Readers who seek more detailed information are referred to Volumes 1 and 5 of *An Illustrated History of LMS Locomotives* by R. J. Essery and David Jenkinson (Oxford Publishing Co, 1981 and Silver Link Publishing Ltd, 1989), which treat this aspect in as much detail as practicable, while frankly admitting areas where intensive study has been unsuccessful.

Changes during Production

Design changes were normally introduced into successive batches of each class, as defined by Works Order Numbers. However it was not infallible; as an example, of the 10 boilers built at Crewe for Derby-built Fairburn 2-6-4Ts to Works Order No 0/672 (Nos 2223-2232) rocking grates were

Below:
No 44766 (Crewe, 12/47) at Willesden in May 1963. Built with Timken roller bearing axleboxes throughout and double-chimney of standard height. Originally fitted with electric lighting equipment. *D. P. Williams*

Below:
Nos 40128 (Derby, 9/35) and 42969 (Crewe, 1/34) at Birkenhead Woodside. *K. Field*

introduced on the last four only — and of course incorporated in all subsequent orders.

Modifications

This covers physical changes carried out retrospectively which were externally visible. Many others were made which were not readily seen. They were invariably carried out during works overhauls. One other modification, which was common to most classes, began in the late 1950s; this was the fitting of BR AWS (Automatic Warning System) equipment. The receiver was mounted on the leading bogie or bissel truck, the most visible sign being a protection plate under the front buffer beam to avoid damage to the receiver from any swing of the screw coupling. There was also an equipment case and two reservoirs, one smaller than the other. Layouts varied according to the available space, but on tender locomotives the equipment case was usually mounted in front of the cab on the right-hand running plate, with one reservoir on each side of the locomotive close by. On tank locomotives this equipment was mounted elsewhere and was not on view. A cable conduit was led along the platform valance angle from the receiver to the cab. This work was done with varying degrees of priority, and so far as is known no Class 3 2-6-2Ts were fitted.

The three-cylinder 2-6-4Ts were refitted after World War 2 with the Hudd automatic train control equip-

ment used on the Tilbury section, from which BR AWS was developed, and retained this until withdrawal; the visual sign was the receiver mounted on the rear bogie, and there was no protection plate below the buffer beam.

Commencing about 1960, provision was made on all locomotives of safety warnings and precautions for working on lines electrified on the 25kV overhead system. Warning 'flash' signs were applied at points where enginemen might climb to dangerous levels. Later the top lamp brackets fitted on smokebox doors and bunkers were moved down (the front brackets to a position on the left-hand side of the door above the bottom hinge-strap) and the centre bracket above the buffer beam was moved to the left to retain the one-over-one headlamp code.

In the last five years or so of steam, various unofficial modifications were made, both in works and at running sheds, to keep locomotives running under rapidly worsening conditions. As examples, many Fairburn 2-6-4Ts and some members of other classes, had the self-cleaning smokebox screens, and the 'SC' plates on the smokebox doors, removed to facilitate tube cleaning. Similarly, most exhaust steam injectors had the large exhaust steam pipe removed and the front of the injector blanked off, confining them to live steam operation only.

These modifications will not be repeated in the text.

Class 3 - 2-6-2T

History

In 1930 Fowler brought out a 2-6-2T design with axleload restricted to 16 tons, intended for stopping and branch line passenger services and short-distance freight work. They were fairly long for their power, since they retained the standard Midland coupled axle spacing of 8ft 0in + 8ft 6in. They proved very unsatisfactory; undersized in the boiler and inexcusably obsolete in the design of the cylinders, valve gear and axleboxes; they certainly did not warrant their power classification 3. Twenty were fitted with condensing gear for working over the 'Widened Lines' to Moorgate with suburban passenger trains, a duty on which they struggled. The rest were confined to light branch line trains and empty carriage workings. The last 10 examples (Nos 61-70), built in 1932 after Stanier's arrival, incorporated certain mechanical improvements in line with his normal practice, but these did nothing for their performance.

With a continuing need for locomotives of this power and versatility, Stanier sought to redesign them in accordance with his own ideas while keeping within the same overall concept and principal dimensions. In little over three years a total of 138 locomotives of the class was built, 113 at Derby and 25 at Crewe. They were still poor locomotives, with inadequate boiler power, and were undoubtedly Stanier's least successful design.

Features

The same wheelbase as that of the Fowler version was retained; it could with advantage have been reduced by 18in or more. Cylinders with extended valve chests and long-travel Walschaerts valve gear overcame the weaknesses of the Fowler design in this respect. The coupling rods were of rectangular section and bearing sizes were generally improved.

The very slender-looking boiler (Class 6A) was sharply tapered and domeless, the top-feed fittings being covered by a small dome-like casing with side bulges. There was a very small superheater of only seven elements which did nothing to improve the steaming.

The double side-window cab with bunker narrowed at the top gave much better weather protection and visibility for the enginemen, but the side tanks were on the shallow side and their limited water capacity sometimes restricted their working range. They weighed 0.75 ton more than the parallel boiler version.

Allocation

These locomotives were distributed widely throughout England, Wales and Scotland, but were employed on a wide range of relatively undemanding work in the fields of stopping passenger and empty carriage working. They were even used for a time on banking duties on the Highland main line, but did not have the staying power for such work. The largest individual allocations were to Stoke, Birkenhead, Kentish Town (London), Nottingham and Dawsholm (Glasgow).

Changes during Production

1 Beginning with No 91 (Derby, 5/35) a pair of washout inspection doors, under small domed covers, was provided each side of the top shoulders of the Belpaire firebox.
2 Starting with No 111 (Derby, 7/35) the cranked and domed vent pipes on top of the side tanks were suppressed in favour of plain pipes clipped to the cab front between the window and firebox each side, extending to the roof.
3 With the building of No 145 (Derby, 7/37) the boiler was modified to match Stanier's second phase thinking. While the diameters were unchanged, the firebox was length-

ened by 6in at foundation ring level, increasing the grate area. A dome was provided in addition to the top-feed; the latter was covered by the later slender casing. The atomiser steam cock, which had been on the left side of the smokebox above the handrail and beneath an elongated cover, was moved to a position below the vacuum ejectors, with no cover.
4 Also from No 145 the opening in the side tanks for the trailing sandbox fillers was done away with, the filler cap being directly on top of the sandbox. Steam standing gear was fitted in lieu of the previous dry trickle sanding.

Modifications

1 In June 1937 No 87 was given a new boiler of the later domed type, and Nos 114 and 139 were similarly modified in 1938. This provided a small pool of spare domeless boilers for exchange at general repairs. A further example, No 83, was modified in the same way in 1943.
2 From about 1938 a start was made on replacing the dry trickle sanding equipment on Nos 71-144 by steam sanding.
3 At about this period the domed tank vent pipes were removed from some (but by no means all) of the locomotives originally fitted, Nos 71-90. They were replaced by plain pipes on the cab front.
4 In 2/41 No 163 was rebuilt with larger boiler (Class 6B) to improve performance. This used the same longer firebox of those on Nos 145-209 but the barrel diameter at the smokebox end was increased from 4ft 2in to 4ft 6in. This allowed the superheater to be doubled in size from seven to 14 elements. A shorter chimney was fitted. This large boiler was pitched with its centreline almost 3in higher above rail. The atomiser steam cock was moved up to a position between the handrail and the ejector exhaust pipe, with no cover.

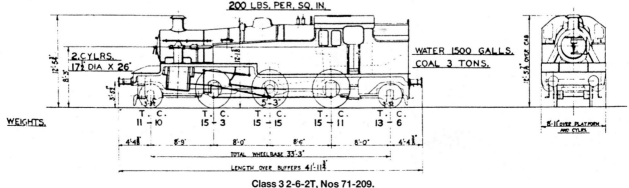

Class 3 2-6-2T, Nos 71-209.

Three further examples (Nos 148/69, 203) were rebuilt in the same way in 1941/42 and surprisingly, two more (Nos 142/67) were given the larger boilers in 1956. While performance should have improved considerably, it is difficult to confirm this since the locomotives remained on relatively lowly jobs.

5 In the late 1940s an attempt was started to improve the steaming of the small Class 6A boiler by more effective draughting. New annular blastpipes were fitted in conjunction with chimneys of larger diameter. All members of the class were so modified at works repairs. The improvement was no more than marginal, and did not overcome the basic inadequacy of the boiler itself.

6 While some of the class were given electrification 'flash' warnings from about 1960, the top lamp brackets were not moved.

Power Classification

When built, all were classed 3P and so marked below the cab windows. Under

BR in 1951 they were redesignated as mixed traffic and classified 3MT, but only the figure 3 was applied, on the bunker side above the number.

Livery

All were built with the LMSR secondary passenger/mixed traffic livery of black lined out in red, though during World War 2 the lining was not renewed. From 1949 BR applied its mixed traffic livery of black, lined out in red, cream and grey, with the crest appropriate at the time.

Withdrawal

The first of the class to be withdrawn were No 40139 (small boiler) and No 40169 (large boiler), both in October 1959. The last surviving 12 (Nos 150/1/3/9/76/7/86-9/96, 200) were condemned in December 1962.

Preserved Locomotives

Nil.

LMSR Nos 71-209

BR Nos 40071-40209

Orders and Construction

Nos	Builder	Lot No	Order No	Building Dates
71-90	Derby	117	8638	02/35-04/35
91-110	Derby	126	8880	05/35-07/35
111-144	Derby	126	8882	07/35-11/35
145-159	Derby	139	9696	07/37-10/37
160-174	Derby	139	9710	10/37-01/38
185-199	Crewe	140	E402	10/37-01/38
200-209	Crewe	140	E403	01/38-04/38
175-184	Derby	139	46	03/38-05/38

Principal Dimensions

2 Cylinders: 17½in dia × 26in stroke
Coupled Wheels: 5ft 3in
Boiler Pressure: 200lb/sq in
Grate Area: 17.5sq ft (71-144)
19.2sq ft (145-209)

Tractive Effort: 21,486lb
Weight in Working Order: 71.25 ton
Coal Capacity: 3 ton
Water Capacity: 1,500gal

Below:
No 40184 (Derby, 5/38) on a Nottingham-Mansfield local at Bulwell in the 1950s. The locomotive carries the larger diameter chimney. BR lined black livery with 1949 crest.
P. J. Lynch

Bottom:
No 163 (Derby, 11/37, rebuilt 2/41) at Derby in February 1948, with larger Class 6B boiler, atomiser steam cock between handrail and ejector exhaust pipe. LMSR wartime plain black livery. *J. M. Jarvis*

Class 4 - Two-Cylinder 2-6-4T Long Wheelbase

History

In 1927 Fowler introduced some highly successful parallel boilered 2-6-4T locomotives to handle heavy suburban passenger trains. With an excellent boiler and long-travel Walschaerts valve gear they proved to be very speedy and were more than once timed at 90mph, despite coupled wheels of only 5ft 9in diameter. Clearly this was a design which Stanier could endorse, but which could not be redesigned immediately to incorporate his own ideas. The last 30 locomotives to be built (Nos 2395-2424) in the 1933 Building Programme were therefore modified from the original design as a halfway stage before the taper boiler version could be produced. The more visible changes were the provision of double side-window cabs, wheels with triangular rims and built-up balance weights, and side bolster bogies and bissel trucks.

These locomotives did splendid work on suburban services in the St Pancras, Stoke, Manchester and Glasgow areas, over the Central Wales line and on banking duties from Oxenholme and Tebay on the West Coast main line.

The building of Stanier's taper boiler version began at the end of 1935, and over the next seven years a total of 206 was built, 133 at Derby and 73 by the North British Locomotive Co (Hyde Park works, Springburn). It was originally intended that the first batch of eight, Nos 2537-2544, should be of the three-cylinder type (see page 22) but this was changed after ordering.

Features

The general layout and wheelbase were similar to that of the parallel boiler version, but slightly larger

Above:
Typical duty: No 42544 (Derby, 12/35) on a Bangor-Afonwen local train leaving Caernarvon. *P. J. Lynch*

cylinders with extended valve chests and outside steam pipes were provided. The valve spindle crosshead guides were fitted to the rear valve chest covers instead of on separate frame brackets. Improvements were made to axleboxes and spring gear.

The taper boiler (Class 4) with top-feed (under the usual small dome-like casing with side bulges) was identical with that of the three-cylinder 2-6-4Ts, save only for an increase in the size of the superheater to 18 elements, and the provision of wash-out inspection doors on the top shoulders of the Belpaire firebox, under small domed covers. The smokebox rested on a saddle.

The side tanks and bunker were of riveted construction, the narrow bunker top being tapered inwards at the back end to give the driver better visibility when running bunker first: this resulted in a prominent diagonal fold line in the bunker side plating. The side tanks featured a small access cutout over the expansion links, to reach which a footstep was fitted to the bottom of the motion plate with a grab handle on the footplate valance angle. The double side-window cab had waist-

height doors and was cut away behind the doorway. A similar bi-directional water scoop to that on the Fowler locomotives was fitted below the cab, revealed by the domes in the back of the cab and the additional operating handle behind the driver. Dry trickle sanding equipment was provided.

The class proved very efficient and economical, though when used on unbraked freight trains great care was needed on steep falling gradients because of their limited brake power.

Allocation

These locomotives saw service in most of the major conurbations, notably on passenger services out of Euston (but very little from St Pancras), in the Birmingham and Manchester areas, around Stoke and Leeds, in East Lancashire and the Glasgow/West of Scotland area. The biggest allocations were at Bletchley, Stoke, Newton Heath (Manchester) and Polmadie (Glasgow).

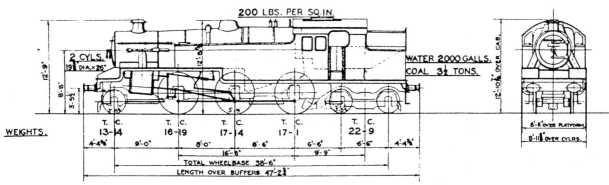

Class 4 2-6-4T, 2-cylinder (long wheelbase), Nos 2425-2494 and 2545-2617.

Above:
The first of the class, No 2537 (Derby, 12/35) when new. It is fitted with domeless boiler, access hole in the side tank, dry trickle sanding, slots in expansion link, and footstep on the motion plate. LMSR lined black livery. *Ian Allan library*

Right:
No 2546 (NBL, 6/36) on a Luton-St Pancras stopping train at Harpenden in August 1936 when new. It has riveted side tanks and bunker, steam sanding, and footstep on the motion plate. LMSR lined black livery with 1936-style sans serif characters. *J. M. Jarvis*

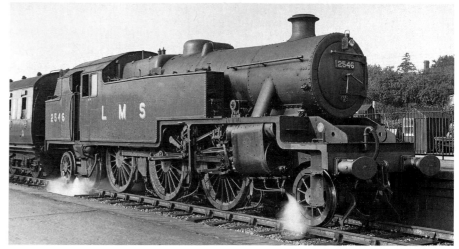

Below:
No 42431 (Derby, 3/36) on Willesden shed in July 1964, running with later domed boiler, access hole in the side tank, steam sanding, lowered top lamp bracket. BR AWS, electrification flashes. BR lined black livery with 1949 crest. *G. N. G. Tingap*

Changes during Production

1 Commencing with No 2425 (Derby, 2/36) a modified boiler was fitted, having a dome separate from the top-feed and a firebox 6in longer at the foundation ring. Those fitted to Derby-built Nos 2425-2494 and North British-built Nos 2545-2617 had 18-element superheaters, while the later examples (Nos 2618-2672) had 21 elements. This made two minor changes in the appearance of the locomotives:

    (i) The atomiser steam cock, which on the first eight had been high on the smokebox (left-hand side) under a pear-shaped casing, was now moved down to a position below the vacuum ejectors, with no cover (but see item 5 below)

    (ii) The cab sides were slightly lengthened to provide a noticeably wider panel between the cab front and the leading window.

2 Also from No 2425 steam sanding equipment replaced the previous dry trickle sanding.

3 From No 2435 (Derby, 3/36) the access holes in the side tanks were suppressed, though the motion plate footsteps remained.

4 The design of the side tanks was adapted to welded rather than riveted construction. It is not known precisely where this change was introduced on North British-built locomotives, but it was no later than No 2607 (12/36). On Derby builds it came in with Nos 2445 (5/36) to 2464 and on Nos 2638 (10/38) to 2672. These welded tanks were not an unqualified success, due to cracking, and all other batches used riveted tanks.

5 With effect from No 2618 (Derby, 6/38) the atomiser steam cock was moved again, being rather higher up between the handrail and the ejector exhaust pipe.

6 Beginning with No 2628 (Derby, 9/38) SKF ball bearings were fitted at the eccentric rod/return crankpin, the enlarged eccentric rod end having a brass cover over the bearings.

LMSR Nos 2425-2494
            2537-2672

Orders and Construction

Nos	Builder	Lot No	Order No	Building Dates
2537-2544	Derby	127	8884	12/35
2425-2444	Derby	128	9204	02/36-05/36
2445-2464	Derby	128	9206	05/36-10/36
2545-2617	North British	133	–	06/36-02/37
2465-2494	Derby	128	9208	10/36-05/37
2618-2627	Derby	144	112	06/38-08/38
2628-2637	Derby	144	114	09/38-10/38
2638-2652	Derby	144	116	10/38-01/39
2653-2662	Derby	148	657	12/40-06/41
2663-2672	Derby	148	660	06/42-02/43

Principal Dimensions

2 Cylinders: 19⅝in dia × 26in stroke
Coupled Wheels: 5ft 9in
Boiler Pressure: 200lb/sq in
Grate Area: 25.0sq ft (2537-2544)
               26.7sq ft (remainder)

Modifications

1 In 1938 work began to replace the dry trickle sanding gear on Nos 2537-2544 by steam sanding.

2 After World War 2 the water pick-up gear, which was blamed for tank bulging, leakage at rivets and cracking at welds, was removed; the domes in the cab remained, however.

3 Some of the 2537-2544 and 2425-2434 batches had the side tank access holes filled in.

4 By 1950 all the motion plate footsteps had been removed; they were perpetually covered in oil and a danger to use. The grab handles on the valance angle were not removed, however, though they now served no useful purpose.

BR Nos 42425-42494
           42537-42672

Tractive Effort: 24,670lb
Weight in Working Order: 87.85 ton
Coal Capacity: 3.5 ton
Water Capacity: 2,000gal

Below:
No 2629 (Derby, 9/38) when new. The locomotive features riveted tanks and bunker, footstep on the motion plate, atomiser steam cock between the handrail and ejector exhaust pipe, and ball bearing eccentric rod end. LMSR lined black livery. *Ian Allan library*

5 In January 1949 one of the domeless batch, No 42538, was modified to take the later standard boiler with longer firebox and dome. No alteration was made to the cab sides, however.

6 In the early 1950s a few examples (eg Nos 42487, 42573) received replacement chimneys of BR standard profile instead of the usual Stanier type.

7 Some 2-6-4Ts were given the small 'top hat' cover on the top-feed casing, suggesting that the new type of clack valve within the boiler cover casting, as on the later Fairburn locomotives, had been fitted. This would have eliminated the clackbox screws which had protruded through the top of the side casings, but this did not always happen; a few sported both the 'top hat' cover *and* the protruding screws at the side!

Power Classification

When built these locomotives were classed 4P and this was painted just below the cab windows. Under BR in 1951 they were redesignated as mixed traffic locomotives and classed 4MT; only the figure 4 was applied on the bunker immediately above the number, though a few had it applied below the cab windows in error.

Livery

The LMSR painted its 2-6-4T locomotives in its secondary passenger livery, black with red lining. The North British-built examples, and some of the 24XX series, were turned out in the 1936 style with sans serif

Above:
No 42573 (NBL, 9/36) on the 16.10 Oxenholme-Windermere stopping train on 4 June 1952, showing riveted tanks and bunker, with chimney to BR Standard profile. LMSR wartime plain black livery. *E. D. Bruton*

characters. During World War 2 and for two or three years after, any repaints omitted the red lining. Very few acquired the 1946-type characters. BR painted them in the standard

Below:
No 42483 (Derby, 2/37) fresh from general repair at Crewe works in May 1958. Clearly visible in this view is the 'top hat' on the top-feed. BR lined black livery with 1957 crest. *G. Wheeler*

black mixed traffic livery with lining in red, grey and cream; on the bunker sides the lining was always applied as a rectangular panel rather then following the cab profile as had been the LMSR practice.

Withdrawal

The first of the class to be withdrawn was No 42490 in May 1960 and the last, No 42616 was condemned in October 1967.

Preserved Locomotives

Nil.

Class 4 - Two-Cylinder 2-6-4T Short Wheelbase

History

By 1943 some 243 2-6-4T locomotives of Stanier design, with either two or three cylinders were in service, having the same 38ft 6in wheelbase as their Fowler predecessors and thus limited to 6 chain minimum radius curves. The accession of C. E. Fairburn as acting CME in 1943 led to a reappraisal of the two-cylinder design, discarding the traditional 8ft 0in+ 8ft 6in coupled wheelbase to give greater flexibility; they could then negotiate 5 chain curves. A bonus was a weight reduction of 2.6 ton.

So successful did this revised design prove that following trials it was also adopted for use on Southern Region services, Brighton works building 41 out of a total of 277. They formed the basis of the BR Standard 2-6-4T (80XXX series), though the latter were less highly regarded by enginemen.

Features

The principal dimensions – apart from length and weight – were unchanged from the Stanier long-wheelbase 2-6-4Ts. There was a considerable number of visual changes, however.

(i) The front platforms were of light folded construction, open in front of the cylinders for easier access to the piston valves
(ii) The side tanks and bunker were of a new design, part welded and part riveted, not supported by a platform valance angle. The internal baffle plates were riveted but the tank bottom was welded as far as the trailing coupled axle, behind which it was riveted. The bunker top had vertical sides and there was an inset footstep
(iii) Footsteps at the front and under the cab were of open type
(iv) The coupling rods were fluted
(v) Double brake blocks articulated on to each hanger were provided to give longer block life
(vi) External sieve boxes were fitted under each tank balancing pipe behind the cab footsteps
(vii) Self-cleaning smokeboxes were fitted. This was not immediately accompanied by the fitting of 'SC' plates below the shed plate
(viii) The atomiser steam cock was moved to the high position on the smokebox as on Nos 2537-2544, and a cover was provided.

Allocation

It would be difficult to name a part of the ex-LMSR system on which these locomotives were not used, from the London area of the Midland Division to the Clyde Coast. Some were allocated to the Tilbury section, running in competition with the three-cylinder Stanier 2-6-4Ts; they did the work

Above:
Typical duty: No 42679 (Derby, 5/45) accelerates a seven-coach Shoeburyness-Fenchurch Street train out of Chalkwell in the early 1950s. *P. J. Lynch*

equally well. For some years each of the Polmadie (Glasgow) locomotives was allocated to two regular crews and they were maintained in almost Royal Train condition – indeed, cleaner than the coaches they hauled!

On the Southern Region they were mainly allocated to Central Division depots, though as electrification spread in the early 1960s they were increasingly displaced to the LM Region.

Changes during Production

1 Starting with No 2223 (Derby, 4/46) the side tanks were altered to eliminate the welding of the tank bottoms. This led to a straight continuous rivet line parallel with the bottom profile of the tank sides.
2 Commencing with No 2229 (Derby, 5/46) all new examples were fitted with rocking grates and hopper ashpans to make shed disposal easier. The operating gear for the ashpan hopper doors projected from the left side

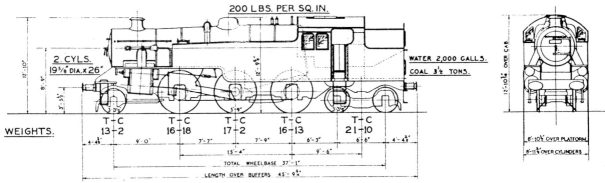

Class 4 2-6-4T, 2-cylinder (short wheelbase), Nos 2187-2199.

Left:
No 2674 (Derby, 4/45) brand-new ex-works, part-welded/part-riveted side tanks and bunker, double brake blocks, external sieve box, footstep on motion plate. LMSR wartime plain black livery. *J. M. Jarvis*

Centre left:
No 42192 (Derby, 1/48) on Beattock shed in the 1950s. Riveted side tanks with straight bottom, self-cleaning smokebox, hopper ashpan, 'top hat' on top-feed. BR lined black livery with 1949 crest. *Ian Allan library*

2200-2222 proved troublesome, and when heavy repairs were needed new riveted bottoms were fitted. This resulted in two steps in the bottom line of rivets, the first a shallow one over the driving axle and the second similar to that on No 2107 onwards.

Power Classification

Originally classed 4P, this was painted on the cab side below the windows (though not on Brighton-built examples). Under BR from 1951 they were redesignated as mixed traffic locomotives and classed 4MT. After a transition period this was shown as '4' above the number on the bunker.

Livery

Being built under wartime or difficult postwar conditions the class emerged in unlined black; some had the 1946-style sans serif characters. Under BR

Below:
No 42080 (Brighton, 1/51) on the Southern Region about 1953. Riveted side tanks with stepped bottom, additional Southern Region headlamp code brackets on smokebox. BR lined black livery with 1949 crest. *W. S. Sellar*

between driving and trailing coupled wheels below the coupling rods.

3 From No 2107 (Derby, 3/49) the tank bottom was changed again to a stepped arrangement, the rivet line being higher over the driving wheels and sloped down to the original level behind the trailing wheels.

4 At about this time the top-feed casings began to incorporate a small 'top hat' cover over the centre section, masking the clackbox securing screws.

5 Brighton-built locomotives were turned out with additional lamp brackets each side of the smokebox to allow Southern Region headcodes (with discs) to be displayed.

Modifications

Essentially there were only two retrospective visual modifications:

1 "Top hat' covers were added to the top-feed casings of earlier locomotives.

2 The original part-welded tank bottoms on Nos 2673-2699 and

this continued for a while, with either 'British Railways' or the 1949 emblem on the side tanks, before the secondary livery of black, lined in red, cream and grey was adopted.

Withdrawal

All the 2-6-4Ts, whether short or long wheelbase, found their work increasingly taken over either by electrification or by the deluge of diesel multiple-units in the late 1950s/early 1960s. The first short wheelbase example was withdrawn in September

1961 (42217) after a life of barely 16 years, and the last nine (Nos 42072/3/85/93, 42138, 42251/2/83, 42689) were withdrawn in September 1967.

LMSR Nos 2187-2189
2200-2299
2673-2699

Preserved Locomotives

Two have been preserved, both on the Lakeside & Haverthwaite Railway. No 2073 (ex-42073) is painted in LNWR black lined livery, similar to but more elaborate than the BR secondary version, while No 2085 (ex-42085) is decked out in pseudo-Caledonian Railway livery of blue, lined in black and white and with Indian red cylinders, etc. Curiously, both survivors are of Brighton build.

BR Nos 42050-42299*
42673-42699

*Construction continued by British Railways

Orders and Construction

Nos	Builder	Lot No	Order No	Building Dates
2673-2677	Derby	177	8277	03/45-05/45
2678-2687	Derby	177	8278	05/45-07/45
2688-2699 } 2200-2202 }	Derby	177	8467	08/45-11/45
2203-2222	Derby	177	8468	11/45-03/46
2223-2232	Derby	185	672	04/46-06/46
2233-2252	Derby	185	675	06/46-11/46
2253-2272	Derby	185	678	11/46-03/47
2273-2292	Derby	186	1676	05/47-11/47
2293-2299 } 2187-42199 }	Derby	186	1678	11/47-03/48
42147-42186	Derby	196	2420	04/48-02/49
42107-42146	Derby	202	3282	03/49-08/50
42096-42106	Brighton	SR3491	—	07/50-10/50
42050-42065	Derby	210	4310	09/50-12/50
42066-42095	Brighton	SR3536	—	10/50-06/51

Principal Dimensions

2 Cylinders: 19⅝in dia × 26in stroke
Coupled Wheels: 5ft 9in
Boiler Pressure: 200lb/sq in
Grate Area: 26.7sq ft

Tractive Effort: 24,670lb
Weight in Working Order: 85.25 ton
Coal Capacity: 3.5 ton
Water Capacity: 2,000gal

Class 4 - Three-Cylinder 2-6-4T

History

The heavy and intensive commuter services on the London, Tilbury & Southend section were, when Stanier arrived in 1932, still being worked almost entirely by saturated 4-4-2Ts of pre-World War 1 LT&SR design. As they became progressively more out-classed on this arduous duty, the LT&SR had bought 4-6-4Ts which proved ineffectual. The Midland Railway, which took over the LT&SR in 1912, had tried its own 0-6-4Ts on these trains, but they were no improvement on the indigenous 4-4-2T. So under LMSR auspices a further 35 LT&SR 4-4-2Ts had been built in 1923, 1925, 1927 and 1930. The Fowler 2-6-4T, which would have revolutionised the train working, could not be used because of weight and hammerblow restrictions over the first three miles out of Fenchurch Street. Stanier was faced with a demand for increased power within these civil engineering restrictions. His solution was a three-cylinder 2-6-4T, an amalgam of the Fowler design, his own thinking as influenced by his Swindon background and the improved balancing and reduced hammerblow of a three-cylinder locomotive, even though this added several tons to the all-up weight. It was also expected that the arrangement would give better starting and acceleration from the many station stops.

Above right:
Typical duty: an eight-coach Fenchurch Street-Tilbury train passes Campbell Road Junction, Bow behind No 42512 (Derby, 7/34) in July 1951. *P. J. Lynch*

Right:
The first of the class, No 2500 (Derby, 4/34) when new. It carries a domeless boiler, domed tank vent pipes, open jawed slidebars with tiebar, rectangular section radius and eccentric rods, dry trickle sanding, full-height cab doors and handrails, vertical bunker top sides. Photographic grey simulation of LMSR lined black livery, power class '4P' high on rear cab side. *Real Photographs*

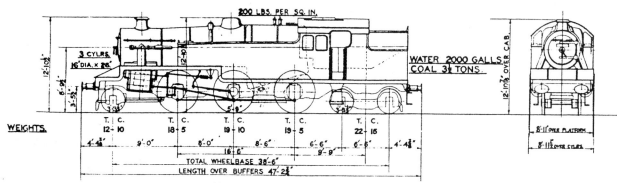

Class 4 2-6-4T, 3-cylinder, Nos 2500-2536.

Above:
No 2508 (Derby, 6/34) at Harpenden in March 1935, with sandbox filler inset in the side tank, LT&S Section destination board brackets, and bunker top sides inclined inwards. LMSR lined black livery. *J. M. Jarvis*

The resultant design proved ideally suited to the difficult conditions on the Tilbury section, and 37 examples were built, displacing many of the 4-4-2Ts to lighter work in other areas.

Features

The three cylinders were in line and all drove the centre coupled axle. Distinguishing features were the narrow cylinder profile, the GWR-style open-jawed slidebars with tiebar between them (as on the first two 'Princesses') and the open-fronted motion plate behind the leading coupled wheels to support them. Side bolster bogies and bissel trucks were fitted. The radius and eccentric rods of the valve gear were unusually of flat rectangular section.

The tapered boiler followed Stanier's early practice in having no steam dome; there was merely the small dome-like casing with side bulges over the top-feed clackboxes. A small superheater of 12 elements only provided moderate superheat. They were the only 2-6-4Ts on which the Stanier hooter was mounted horizontally.

Great emphasis was laid on the comfort of the enginemen, who were given a totally-enclosed double side-window cab with full-height doors containing drop lights. The bunker top section was narrowed to provide an unobstructed lookout when running bunker first without leaning out of the cab.

Allocation

For the first 12 months the initial five members of the class worked on Euston, Broad Street and St Albans suburban services pending the completion of certain bridge work on the Tilbury section. Thereafter all went to the Tilbury section, allocated to Plaistow, Shoeburyness and (the occasional example) Tilbury sheds. There they tackled packed 12-coach trains on sharp timings with frequent stops with great success, and on a dry rail could be driven away from stations in full gear with the regulator fully open. During World War 2 many of them were dispersed to Midland Division depots for (mainly) freight work, leaving the old 4-4-2Ts to soldier on with the heavy Tilbury workings. Two 2-6-4Ts were briefly transferred to Greenock (Ladyburn) in 1951.

Changes during Production

1 Commencing with No 2505 (6/34) tall destination board brackets to suit Tilbury section practice were fitted on the front platform, together with additional brackets on the back of the bunker. Nos 2505-2509 also had an opening in the side tanks for an inset sandbox filler.

2 From No 2510 (6/34) the bunker sides were tapered inwards towards the top of the rear end to improve visibility of close signals and platform ends when running bunker first; this resulted in a diagonal fold line in the side plating. Short footsteps, of two different types, were also provided on the sloping shoulders of the bunker to facilitate the trimming of coal.

3 Beginning with No 2515 (8/34) the radius and eccentric rods were made of fluted section instead of rectangular.

4 Responding to footplate staff complaints that the enclosed cab became too hot (perhaps 1934 was a particularly good summer) No 2525 (9/34) onwards saw the abandonment of full-height cab doors. The usual waist-height folding doors were fitted, and the opening behind the doorway enlarged. Half-height handrails were provided.

Modifications

1 Within a few years all the full-height cab doors on Nos 2500-2524 were cut down to waist height, but the straight rear edge of the doorway was not cut away nor the full-height handrails shortened.

2 Commencing in 1937 the dry trickle sanding equipment was replaced by steam sanding and the back sandpipes to the trailing coupled wheels removed.

3 Three members of the class were provided with domed boilers standard with those on later two-cylinder 2-6-4Ts, with the longer firebox and 18 superheater elements, to provide a pool of spare boilers for exchange at general repairs. They were Nos 2505 (12/37), 2513 (12/37) and 2523 (3/43).

4 In early BR days the cranked and domed vent pipes on top of the side tanks were dispensed with.

5 At about this time also the front destination board brackets were removed. Some of the class at least were given extended footsteps almost the full length of the bunker side shoulders.

6 Following prewar experiments on the LT&S section, which was very prone to fog off the Thames estuary, all of the class were fitted from about 1948 with the Hudd inductive system of automatic train control, a forerunner of the BR AWS system. In this case the receiver unit was visible, mounted below an additional stretcher between the bogie frames at the back end. There was no need to protect it from the swing of the screw coupling.

Power Classification

As-built the locomotives were classed '4P' and so painted below the cab

LMSR Nos 2500-2536   **BR Nos** 42500-42536

Orders and Construction

Nos	Builder	Lot No	Order No	Building Dates
2500-2504	Derby	102	8425	04/34
2505-2536	Derby	116	8503	06/34-12/34

The original intention was to build eight further three-cylinder locomotives of this type, but in the event these eight pioneered the two-cylinder version of the Stanier 2-6-4T.

Principal Dimensions

3 Cylinders: 16in dia × 26in stroke
Coupled Wheels: 5ft 9in
Boiler Pressure: 200lb/sq in
Grate Area: 25.0sq ft

Tractive Effort: 24,598lb
Weight in Working Order: 92.25 ton
Coal Capacity: 3.5 ton
Water Capacity: 2,000gal

windows. From 1951 BR categorised them as mixed traffic locomotives, and the figure 4 was applied above the number on the bunker side.

Livery

Under the LMSR the three-cylinder 2-6-4Ts were painted black with red lining, appropriate for secondary passenger locomotives. After being plain black, unlined during and after World War 2 they received the BR mixed traffic livery of black, lined in red, cream and grey.

Withdrawal

The LT&S line was electrified at 25/6.25kV, and electric services started in November 1961, with full implementation in the summer of 1962. This made the three-cylinder 2-6-4Ts redundant, and withdrawal of locomotives needing works attention

began with No 42512 in November 1960. Seven more were condemned in 1961. All the remaining engines were withdrawn en masse in June 1962.

Preserved Locomotives

No 2500 forms part of the National Collection and is preserved at Bressingham Museum, Norfolk in prewar LMSR lined black livery (which is not applied accurately).

Right:
No 2513 (Derby, 7/34) at Derby in December 1937, newly fitted with domed boiler, steam sanding (not to trailing coupled wheels), and short bunker footstep. LMSR lined black livery. *J. M. Jarvis*

Below right:
No 2536 (Derby, 12/34) when new, with domed tank vent pipes, half-height cab doors and handrails, back cab cut-out, dry trickle sanding. Photographic grey simulation of LMSR lined black livery. *Ian Allan library*

Below:
No 42521 (Derby, 9/34) after general repair, on Derby shed on 10 March 1956. The locomotive has fluted radius and eccentric rods, no tank vent pipes, steam sanding (not to trailing coupled wheels), and a full-length bunker side step. BR lined black livery with 1949 crest. *R. J. Buckley*

Class 5 - 2-6-0

History

The Hughes parallel boiler 2-6-0s (nicknamed 'Crabs') proved to be a highly competent and economical design, and building continued from 1926 to 1932, by which time a fleet of 245 was in service. When 40 more locomotives in this category were authorised in the 1933 Building Programme, Stanier decided to change the design to incorporate his own ideas of higher boiler pressure, modest superheat, a tapered boiler and smaller cylinders which would not need to be so steeply inclined. Much of the design work was done in the Horwich drawing office, and various details betrayed this origin. The 40 locomotives were built in the short period of five months, but were never added to, their role being taken over within months by the new Class 5 4-6-0s.

Features

The boiler was of a similar diameter to those subsequently used on the 'Jubilees' and Class 5, but shorter. The barrel was in two rings, the front one cylindrical and the second tapered, and the boiler clothing reflected this shape. There was neither a dome nor the usual safety valves on the firebox top; instead, the safety valves were combined with the top-feed in a fitting on the boiler barrel, beneath a casing very similar to that on GWR classes. The circular smokebox rested on a cast saddle of much heavier appearance than Stanier's later fabricated saddles.

Because the higher boiler pressure allowed smaller cylinders to be used, these could be horizontal while staying within the loading gauge. They had extended valve chests and the clothing was almost square at the top. A crosshead-driven vacuum pump was mounted below the bottom slidebar on the left-hand side. The wide gap between the cylinder top and the platform accommodated a snifting valve.

A Horwich-style double side-window was fitted, and the class perpetuated the Horwich practice of the front platform being narrower than that over cylinders and motion, a feature which continued on the Class 5 4-6-0s and Class 8F 2-8-0s. Only a single vacuum ejector was provided, the body of which was much smaller than the two-ejector type; it was just in front of the cab on the left side with long exhaust pipe to the smokebox.

A standard Fowler 3,500gal tender, much narrower than the cab, was attached. It had coal rails, but surprisingly no water scoop. The class appeared at a time when snap-head rivets were displacing flush countersunk ones, and both cab and tender exhibited a positive rash of rivet heads.

Out-of-character features for the Stanier marque were the very shallow platform valance angles (a long-standing Horwich practice), the fitting of steam sanding at a time when Stanier had 'imported' dry trickle sanding from Swindon, and the use of

Above:
Typical duty: No 42951 passes Acton Bridge on a down through freight on 31 July 1956.
S. D. Wainwright

a Midland whistle rather than the Caledonian-type hooter.

Allocation

When first built members of the class were allocated to all four LMSR Divisions (including Scotland, where they were used briefly on Glasgow-Aberdeen expresses) but before long they were concentrated on the Western Division, with the largest allocations to Crewe South, Nuneaton and Mold Junction. Their duties were largely confined to freight, though in the summer months they were called on for some weekend passenger and excursion work.

Changes during Production

1 The first change took place before No 13245 was turned into traffic!

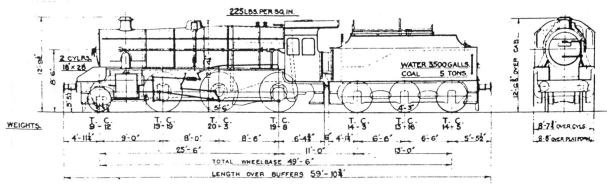

Class 5 2-6-0, Nos 13245-13284.

When Stanier saw the GWR-style 'bonnet' over the top-feed and safety valves in Crewe works yard he ordered its immediate removal, regarding it as too much a copy of Swindon practice. So before entering traffic the first 10 were given a more dome-like cover, though of a tall curiously slender and tapered shape, from the top of which the safety valves just protruded. (The official class photograph purporting to be No 13245 was in fact a much later locomotive masquerading as the original.)

Above:
No 2950 (Crewe, 11/33) at Crewe South shed in 1936. This view shows the boiler clothing parallel at front, tapered behind, with a tall cover over top-feed and safety valves, square-topped cylinder castings, mechanical lubricator drive. Dirty LMSR lined black livery.
Photomatic

2 Commencing with No 13255 (12/33) conventional squat pop safety valves were fitted on the firebox top and the top-feed casing altered to the flatter mini-dome with side bulges which became the early Stanier hall-mark. The boiler clothing remained part-parallel, part-tapered.
3 Also beginning with No 13255 a new design of cylinder casting with rounded top was adopted. The tenders were also fitted with water pick-up gear.

Below:
No 2950 in the late 1930s fresh from general repair. The boiler clothing is now altered to uniform taper, with hinged glass windshields on the cab, still classed '5P4F'. LMSR lined black livery. *P. Ransome-Wallis*

4 From No 13265 (1/34) the boiler clothing was uniformly tapered.

5 At some point between Nos 13266 (1/34) and 13270, hinged glass draught screens were fitted on the driver's side of the cab only. Relenting this parsimony, draught screens were fitted to both sides from No 13275 (1/34).

6 Nos 13280-13284 were built with only one mechanical lubricator on the right-hand running plate — for the axleboxes — instead of two. The cylinders were looked after by a sight feed lubricator in the cab.

Modifications

1 From about 1936 hinged glass draught screens were fitted to both sides of the cab where these had not been provided from new. The work seems never to have been completed.

2 In the late 1930s, at first general repair, the boiler clothing of Nos 2945-2964 was altered to show a uniform taper.

Below:
No 2973 (Crewe, 1/34) at Nuneaton shed about 1938, with safety valves on the firebox top, dome-like top-feed cover, round-topped cylinder castings, and washout inspection doors on the firebox shoulders, classed '5'. Grimy LMSR lined black livery. B. E. Thomas

3 From 1938 the vacuum pumps were removed and the single vacuum ejectors replaced by the normal double type.

4 The 10 boilers built with combined top-feed and safety valves were altered to the later standard in the 1940s and 1950s, the tall top-feed casings being replaced by the more squat pattern. However, they were generally recognisable by the side bulges on the top-feed casing, which had a flattened face.

LMSR Nos 13245-13284
(from 1934) 2945-2984

Orders and Construction

Nos	Builder	Lot No	Order No	Building Dates
13245-13254	Crewe	104	E372	10/33-12/33
13255-13264	Crewe	104	E373	12/33-01/34
13265-13274	Crewe	104	E374	01/34
13275-13284	Crewe	104	E375	01/34-03/34

Principal Dimensions

2 Cylinders: 18in dia × 28in stroke
Coupled Wheels: 5ft 6in
Boiler Pressure: 225lb/sq in
Grate Area: 27.8sq ft
Tractive Effort: 26,288lb

Power Classification

For some reason, when new the 2-6-0s were designated as freight locomotives and carried the classification '4F' above the cab windows, despite the fact that their parallel boiler predecessors were already carrying dual passenger/freight markings. In 1934 this was changed to '5P4F' as on the Hughes 2-6-0s, and in the late 1930s it was changed again to '5P5F'. At about the time of Nationalisation they were

BR Nos 42945-42984

Weight in Working Order:
  Locomotive: 69.1 ton
  Tender: 42.2 ton
  Total: 111.3 ton
Coal Capacity: 5 ton
Water Capacity: 3,500gal

Above:
No 42959 (Crewe, 1/34) at Mold Junction about 1955. It has no washout inspection doors on firebox shoulders, a dome-like top-feed casing with flattened side covers, round-topped cylinder castings, and hinged glass cab windshields. BR lined black livery with 1949 crest. *D. Penney*

reclassified '6P5F', but this was unrealistic for their capabilities and so far as is known none was so painted. Some even reverted to '5F' with no passenger class. From 1949 BR unambiguously categorised them as mixed traffic locomotives, power class 5MT, which was shown on the cab side above the number without suffix.

Livery

The LMSR painted the 2-6-0s black with red lining, belying their original freight category. During World War 2 and for a few years after the lining was not renewed. Under BR they received the mixed traffic livery of black, lined in red, grey and cream.

Withdrawal

The first of the class to be withdrawn was No 42976 in July 1963. Heavy scrapping did not start until the end of 1965, but was completed in July 1966 with No 42963.

Preserved Locomotives

Only one of the class has been preserved, No 2968, which has recently been overhauled at Bridgnorth (Severn Valley Railway) and is once again in LMS black livery.

Class 5 - 4-6-0

History

When Stanier arrived on the LMSR the only modern general purpose mixed traffic locomotive in the fleet was the Hughes 2-6-0. Excellent in a freight role, its speed capabilities in passenger service were limited both by the 5ft 6in wheels and by some hesitation about the adequacy of guidance given by a leading bissel truck at high speeds. With experience of the GWR 'Hall' class 4-6-0s behind him, Stanier specified a design with virtually the same principal dimensions, but incorporating much proven LMSR technology and his own inclinations. They were to be utterly simple in design but with the best modern features.

So successful did this concept prove that construction continued for more than 16 years and ultimately led to a total of 820 locomotives (plus 22 variants with poppet valve gear). 393 were built in railway works and 427 by private builders, including the largest single order ever placed by a British railway, for 227 locomotives from Armstrong Whitworth & Co.

Numbers started at 5000, but unusually the first of the class was No 5020 (8/34) built by Vulcan Foundry, which preceded the first of the Crewe-built locomotives by six months. Clearly, building in large numbers was envisaged from the start and a block of 500 numbers was allocated. In practice this proved quite inadequate and it became necessary to backtrack with numbers first to 4800, then into a 47XX series and finally into a 46XX series. In addition there was considerable out-of-sequence building by different building works.

Features

The cylinders had extended valve chests to give straight ports. The Walschaerts valve gear had the Horwich style of cranked flat-section combination lever, union link and crosshead arm secured by two bolts, as

Above:
No 44830 (Crewe, 8/44) pulls out of Bournemouth West on an afternoon stopping train for Bath in the early 1950s. Note the unique S&DJ passenger headlamp code.
P. J. Lynch

on the 2-6-0s. A crosshead-driven vacuum pump was mounted under the left-hand bottom slidebar. Coupling rods were of flat rectangular section. The front platform was some 10½in narrower than that over cylinders and coupled wheels, a feature which, together with the absence of splashers, made them readily distinguishable from the rather similar 'Jubilees'. Both mechanical lubricators were mounted on the right-hand platform over the driving axle. Dry trickle sanding was provided.

The boiler has a tapered barrel and gently rounded Belpaire firebox. Because the throatplate was straight the visible transition from boiler barrel to firebox was about 1ft behind the driving axle. There was no dome, only a top-feed with small dome-like cover similar to that introduced on the later 2-6-0s. The pipes to it were prominent under covers outside the boiler clothing. The modest super-

heater comprised 14 elements. A rather tall chimney with straight sides was fitted, reaching to 12ft 10½in above rail.

The double side-window cab differed from that on the 2-6-0s in having a straight rear edge with no cut-out. Both large and small vacuum ejectors were provided, just in front of the cab and with long exhaust pipe to the smokebox. The new standard 4,000gal tender, with the side sheets rolled inwards at the top over the bunker, was attached.

Allocation

The first of the class, No 5020, was used on the Western Division, but the

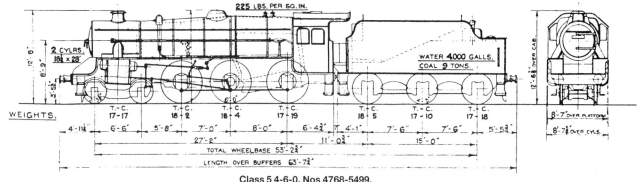

Class 5 4-6-0, Nos 4768-5499.

Above:
No 45345 (AW, 4/37) runs into Oxenholme with a through freight from the Windermere branch on 13 June 1950. The locomotive has unusually been fitted at repair with a tall chimney.
E. D. Bruton

Centre right:
First of the class, No 5020 (VF, 8/34) when new. It is fitted with a domeless straight throatplate boiler, tall chimney, Horwich-style crosshead arm, vacuum pump, dry trickle sanding, and riveted tender tank. LMSR lined black livery.
Ian Allan library

Bottom right:
No 5032 (VF, 9/34) passes Yate on an up express in 1935, with feed pipes to the top-feed outside clothing, and no front step cover under the smokebox front. LMSR lined black livery.
L&GRP

next nine went to Perth for use on the Highland section, where they revolutionised the train working. As further examples came into service their geographical operations spread until they were to be seen on almost the entire system, from London to Oban and Wick and from Bournemouth and Swansea to York. Only two destinations, Stranraer and Kyle of Lochalsh, were barred to them for some years, in each case by inadequate turntables.

Changes during Production

Inevitably in such a numerous class as the 'Black 5', where building continued under three CMEs over a long period, a large number of design changes was made in a continuous search for improvements. From 1943

onwards such changes could be introduced in two separate orders emerging simultaneously from two works; in some cases, therefore, it has been necessary to quote two locomotive numbers as the first to be modified.

1 Commencing in the first Vulcan Foundry order in October 1934 (the precise locomotive cannot now be traced but is thought to have been No 5042 of 10/34) a raised step cover was fitted on the front platform in front of the smokebox saddle to give easier access to the top lamp bracket. This became standard for all future builds.

2 Nos 5000 (Crewe, 2/35) to 5019 and Nos 5070 (Crewe, 5/35) to 5074 were built with steam heating connections at the front buffer beam, whereas the Vulcan Foundry-built Nos 5020 (8/34) to 5069 and 5075 (2/35) to 5124 had no front connections. Nor did the first 100 from Armstrong Whitworth, Nos 5125 to 5224, have them.

3 From No 5000 and 5075 (VF, 2/35) a new design of chimney was fitted which was arguably more shapely; it was 2½in shorter, giving a height above rail of 12ft 8in on most locomotives. This was also standardised for future builds.

4 Also with effect from Nos 5070 (Crewe, 5/35) and 5075 (VF, 2/35) details of the Walschaerts valve gear were altered. The Horwich-style

Left:
No 5225 (AW, 8/36) new outside the builder's works in Newcastle upon Tyne. It has a sloping throatplate boiler with dome, Derby-type crosshead arm with three-stud fastening, and steam sanding. LMSR lined black livery with 1936 sans serif characters including '5P5F' power classification. *Ian Allan library*

Centre left:
No 44810 (Derby, 10/44) at Leeds Holbeck shed in May 1961, with 10ft 10in connecting rods with longer union links, double articulated brake blocks, fixed cab front side windows, and ball bearing eccentric rod end. BR lined black livery with 1957 crest and electrification flashes. *G. W. Morrison*

Bottom left:
No 44929 (Crewe, 3/46) on Newton Heath shed in May 1960. It is seen with a boiler with forward top-feed (not as-built), 'top hat' on top-feed casing, no SC indication, lower atomiser steam cock, hopper ashpan operating gear, part-welded/part-riveted tender tank, and modified tender spring links. BR lined black livery with 1957 crest. *J. E. Wilkinson*

cranked flat section combination lever was replaced by a straight fluted lever with slight offset, but it was still forked at the bottom pin, allowing use of the same union link and crosshead arm secured to the crosshead by two bolts.

5 At the same time two washout inspection doors were provided each side on the top shoulders of the Belpaire firebox, masked by small domed covers.

6 Also from Nos 5000 and 5070 the injector delivery pipes to the top-feed were altered to lie flush in the boiler clothing and covered by a flat strip.

7 Beginning with Nos 5007 (Crewe, 3/35) and 5075 (VF, 2/35) the superheater was increased in size to 21 elements, following dynamometer car tests in October 1934 which showed that low superheat was not conducive to good economy; this did not affect the locomotive's appearance.

8 No 5125 (AW, 5/35) was the first of the class provided with a 4,000gal tender tank of welded construction rather than riveted. This saved nearly half a ton in weight.

9 On the second Armstrong Whitworth order commencing with No 5225 (8/36) a major redesign of the boiler took place. The firebox was lengthened by fitting a sloping throatplate, which brought the boiler barrel/firebox transition forward virtually to the centreline of the driving axle; at the grate the firebox was no longer. A dome was provided immediately in front of the firebox and the top-feed moved forward a little, now under a more slender casing. The superheater was further enlarged to 24 elements. This boiler, with minor variations, was used on all future builds.

10 A further redesign of the valve gear took place at the same time. The straight fluted combination lever was modified at the bottom pin to suit a union link forked at each end; a new Derby-style crosshead arm was fitted, with three-stud fastening to the crosshead.

11 No 5225 also introduced steam sanding to the class instead of the dry trickle sanding. It also reintroduced a steam heating connection on the front buffer beam, provided on all future Class 5s. No design changes were made in the course of this 227-strong order.

12 From No 5452 (Crewe, 9/38) the superheater was increased further in size to 28 elements, which became the future standard. At the same time SKF ball bearings were introduced for the eccentric rod/return crankpin, the rod end being enlarged and bearings sealed by a circular brass cover. This, too, became the future standard.

13 Another more subtle change came in with No 5452. Hitherto both cab side-windows, clearly visible in wooden frames, had been of the sliding type, but now the front window was fixed and the wooden frame dispensed with. The beadings round the cab window openings, which had been of half-round section and with radiused bottom corners, gave way to flat beadings with square bottom corners.

14 The crosshead-driven vacuum pump was omitted from No 5452 and all subsequent examples, and the profile of the crosshead modified to suit.

15 Lastly No 5452 saw the introduction on this class of twin brake blocks articulated on the hangers.

16 No 5472 (Derby, 4/43) introduced further changes to the motion arrangement. The connecting rods were shortened from 11ft 3in to 10ft 10in centres and the piston rods and union links lengthened by 5in to compensate. This was done to enable the piston head to be drawn clear of the cylinder without 'breaking' the piston rod joint to the crosshead for changing piston rings. This resulted in two readily visible changes: the length of the union link was much greater and the slidebars projected further behind the motion plate. In addition a new design of coupling rod was adopted, fluted instead of rectangular in section and slightly fish-bellied. These changes became standard for the future.

17 From Nos 4826 (Crewe, 7/44) and 4807 (Derby, 9/44) the valve spindle crosshead guides were changed from rather solid-looking non-ferrous castings to an open-looking steel fabricated design of flat guides spaced by bobbins.

18 From the same numbers, alterations were made to the tender tanks. The all-welded form had brought some problems with seam fractures, and

Below:
Coal weighing tender No 10591 (Horwich, 8/46) attached to No 4966 when new. The tender features a part-welded/part-riveted tank, water sieve box below tank, narrow bunker, relieving gear alongside, steelyard casing between bunker and pick-up dome, and modified spring links. LMSR plain black livery. *Ian Allan library*

so part-welded construction was adopted, with the internal baffle plates riveted to the side, rear and base plates. All future tenders used this construction method; they could be distinguished from the fully riveted tenders by the lack of horizontal lines of rivets immediately above the base and at tank top level.

19 In 1944, it is believed from No 4826 (Crewe, 7/44) the atomiser steam cock was moved from a position above the handrail to a lower position between the handrail and the ejector exhaust pipe.

20 From either No 4846 (Crewe, 11/44) or 4856 (12/44) the tender spring links were modified. The top pin rested in a deeper shoe on the end of the spring but instead of passing through a frame bracket, with a cylindrical casing at the bottom (containing rubber springs) and an adjusting nut, the link was secured in a modified frame bracket by a single pin.

21 With effect from Nos 4856 (Crewe, 12/44) and 4932 (Horwich, 9/45) self-cleaning smokeboxes were fitted, with internal baffle plates and screens to reduce servicing. The only visible change was the 'SC' indication on the smokebox door, originally painted above the shed plate but quickly replaced by a cast plate below the shed plate.

22 Nos 4922 (Crewe, 1/46) and 4948 (Horwich, 2/46) were the first of the class fitted with rocking grates and hopper ashpans for easier servicing on the ashpit. Apart from the shape of the ashpan, the hopper door operating gear was visible between driving and trailing coupled wheels on the left-hand side below the coupling rods.

23 Two coal weighing tenders were built in 1946 and attached to Nos 4966 (Horwich, 8/46) and 4986 (Horwich, 10/46) when new. These had been requested by the Motive Power Depart-

ment to enable them to carry out simple coal consumption tests and demonstrations. In later years they were paired with other locomotives. The bunker was narrower than the tank, straight-sided and with covers at the side over the relieving gear and at the back over the weighing steelyard. Tank capacity was reduced to 3,750gal. These tenders also had small external sieve boxes attached to the tank bottom on each side between leading and intermediate axleboxes.

24 No 44997 (Horwich, 3/47) introduced a modified form of the sloping throatplate boiler, in which the top-feed was moved forward on to the front ring of the boiler barrel. All future boilers built were of this type, though in Scotland they were often switched on to earlier locomotives at general repairs.

Below:
Coal weighing tender No 10591 in the early 1960s attached to No 45298, with the weighing equipment and steelyard casing removed, and fire iron tunnel added on bunker side.
M. G. Martin

Above:
No 4758 (Crewe, 9/47) when new. It has Timken roller bearings with longer wheelbase, boiler barrel/firebox transition slightly behind driving axle, circular tender axlebox covers, and tender sieve box between leading and intermediate axleboxes. Photographic grey simulation of LMSR plain black livery with 1946 sans serif characters. *Ian Allan library*

25 Also starting with No 44997 the standard external sieve boxes appeared on the tender and were fitted to all subsequent builds; they allowed the sieve screens to be cleaned without emptying the tank of water. They were larger than those on the coal weighing tenders and mounted on a plate spanning the D-shaped frame opening between leading and intermediate axleboxes, not directly attached to the tank bottom.

26 Nos 4758 (Crewe, 9/47) to 4767 were fitted with Timken roller bearing axleboxes throughout. Those on the locomotive were not readily visible, but the tender bearings were easily identified by the circular axlebox covers in place of the rectangular

Above:
No 4767 (Crewe, 12/47) when new. This one-off locomotive has Timken roller bearings with longer coupled wheelbase, and Stephenson valve gear. LMSR plain black livery with 1946 characters, power class '5'. *Ian Allan library*

ribbed covers of plain bearing axle-boxes. In order to accommodate the wider axleboxes in front of the firebox the wheelbase between driving and trailing axles was increased from 8ft 0in to 8ft 4in. This set the boiler barrel/firebox transition back 4in behind the centreline of the driving axle and lengthened the smokebox by the same amount. All subsequent examples, whether with or without roller bearings, were built to this longer wheelbase.

27 Three of the class, Nos 4765-4767 (Crewe, 12/47) were built with electric lighting equipment. The Stone turbo-generator was mounted low down on the right-hand side of the smokebox, with small lamp housings at each head and tail position front and rear alongside or above the usual lamp bracket.

28 Nos 4765-4767 were also fitted with double chimneys of standard height.

29 No 4767 (Crewe, 12/47) was unique in being fitted with outside Stephenson valve gear instead of the standard Walschaerts gear; it was driven from double-return cranks with (unusually, since the Hughes 2-6-0s) square fixing with through bolts to the crankpin. The eccentric rods had plain bearings rather than the ball bearings of contemporary Walschaerts-fitted examples; the forward (inner) rods had split rear

bearings. The drive to the mechanical lubricators on the right-hand side was by a linkage from the rear end of the backward (outer) eccentric rod.

30 No 44658 (Crewe, 5/49) was also turned out with Stone electric lighting equipment.

31 The last 38 examples, Nos 44658 (Crewe, 5/49) to 44667, 44668 (Horwich, 12/49) to 44685 and 44688 (Horwich, 8/50) to 44697 had small 'top hat' covers on top of the top-feed casing to clear the clackbox retaining screws in the later type of top-feed casting.

32 In 1949 and 1950 there were further experimental installations of roller bearing axleboxes. Nos 44668 (Horwich, 12/49) to 44677 were fitted with SKF axleboxes on the driving axle only, but this did not affect the appearance of the locomotive in any way. Nos 44678 (Horwich, 5/50) to 44685 were given SKF axleboxes throughout, and this was evident in the circular covers of the tender axleboxes. Lastly Nos 44688 (Horwich, 8/50) to 44697 were fitted with Timken roller bearings on the driving axle only, again without visible change.

33 Two further coal weighing tenders were built and coupled to Nos 44677 (Horwich, 4/50) and 44696 (Horwich, 12/50) when new. They were similar to but not identical with the first two; the bunker held slightly

more coal and the steelyard casing was smaller. These tenders also were paired with other locomotives in later years.

Modifications

These were numerous and complex, and are almost impossible to catalogue accurately after many years. The following notes cover as far as practicable the visual changes.

Nos 5000-5224 (built with straight throatplate boilers)

1 The 57 boilers originally built with small (14-element) superheaters were modified at first general repair (1936-40); they were given 24-element superheaters together with domes. The top-feed position was not altered but casings of the later type were fitted. These boilers were then available for use on any of the 212 which had not been modified in accordance with item 3 below.

2 Four Class 5s allocated to Scottish depots were given regimental names in 1936/37. The cast brass nameplates were curved, with crest above, and carried on a mock splasher above the

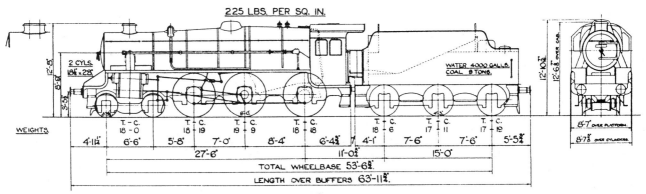

225 LBS. PER SQ. IN.

Class 5 4-6-0, roller bearings, Nos 4758-4766.

LMSR Nos 4758-5499

BR Nos 44658-44685*
44688-44737*
44758-45499
*Construction continued by British Railways

Note: In this book the 'standard' Class 5 4-6-0s – which in practice were anything but standard – are divided into two groups:
  (i) the piston valve locomotives, all with Walschaerts valve gear except for one with Stephenson valve gear,
  (ii) those fitted with British Caprotti poppet valve gear, and dealt with separately

Orders and Construction

Nos	Builder	Lot No	Order No	Building Dates
5020–5069	Vulcan Foundry	119	–	08/34-01/35
5000-5019	Crewe	114	E377	02/35/05/35
5075-5124	Vulcan Foundry	123	–	02/35-07/35
5070-5074	Crewe	122	E393	05/35-12/35
5125-5224	Armstrong Whitworth	124	–	05/35-12/35
5225-5451	Armstrong Whitworth	131	–	08/36-12/37
5452-5461	Crewe	142	E405	09/38-10/38
5462-5471	Crewe	142	E406	11/38-12/38
5472-5481	Derby	151	3836	04/43-09/43
5482-5491	Derby	152	4141	09/43-12/43
5492-5499 4800-4806 }	Derby	153	4888	01/44-07/44
4826-4835	Crewe	170	E453	07/44-09/44
4836-4845	Crewe	170	E454	09/44-10/44
4807-4825	Derby	170	8283	09/44-12/44
4846-4855	Crewe	170	E455	11/44-12/44
4856-4865	Crewe	170	E456	12/44-02/45
4866-4871	Crewe	170	E457	02/45-03/45
4872-4891	Crewe	174	E458	03/45-08/45
4892-4911	Crewe	174	E459	09/45-11/45
4932-4941	Horwich	174	95	09/45-12/45
4912-4931	Crewe	174	E460	11/45-04/46
4942-4966	Horwich	174	96	12/45-08/46
4967-4981	Crewe	183	E463	04/46-07/46
4982-4996	Horwich	183	97	09/46-02/47
4997-4999 4783-4789 }	Horwich	187	98	03/47-05/47
4768-4782	Crewe	187	E466	04/47-08/47
4790-4799	Horwich	187	99	06/47-10/47
4758-4767	Crewe	187	E467	09/47-12/47
44698-44717	Horwich	192	102	07/48-12/48
44728-44737 44718-44727 }	Crewe	192	E472	01/49-05/49
44658-44667	Crewe	199	E473	05/49-07/49
44668-44685 44688-44697 }	Horwich	199	105	12/49-12/50

Principal Dimensions

2 Cylinders: 18½in dia × 28in stroke
Coupled Wheels: 6ft 0in
Boiler Pressure: 225lb/sq in
Grate Area: 27.8sq ft (5000-5224)
          28.65sq ft (5225 onwards)
Tractive Effort: 25,455lb

Weight in Working Order:
  Locomotive: 72.1 ton to 75.3 ton
  Tender: 53.15 ton to 54.1 ton
  Total: 125.25 ton to 129.4 ton
Coal Capacity: 9 ton
Water Capacity: 4,000gal

leading coupled wheels. The names selected were:
  5154 *Lanarkshire Yeomanry*
  5156 *Ayrshire Yeomanry*
  5157 *The Glasgow Highlander*
  5158 *Glasgow Yeomanry*
It was the intention to name No 5155 *Queens Edinburgh*, but this was not done. These four remained the only named Class 5s during LMSR/BR service.

3 In order to provide a pool of spare straight throatplate boilers for exchange at general repairs, modifi-

cations were made to the frames and stretcher in front of the firebox on 13 locomotives to allow sloping throatplate boilers with domes to be fitted. Those modified were Nos 5002/20/2/3/6/7/40/7/54/7/8/97 and 5142, during 1937/38.

4 The first 20-odd Vulcan Foundry-built examples, turned out without the step cover in front of the smokebox saddle were fitted in the late 1930s.

5 The taller chimneys fitted new to Nos 5020-5069 were replaced by chimneys of the shorter standard height,

Above:
No 44737 (Crewe, 3/49) at Crewe works after general repair in March 1959. Features include: longer coupled wheelbase with plain bearings, 'SC' plate, and 'top hat' on top-feed casing. BR lined black livery with 1957 crest. *K. R. Pirt*

usually at first general repair, though at least one, No 5068, retained its tall chimney for some years after being fitted with a domed boiler.

6 Dry trickle sanding was replaced by steam sanding equipment from 1937 onwards.

7 All vacuum pumps were removed from 1938 onwards.

Other locomotives

8 Vacuum pumps were removed from Nos 5225-5451 from 1938 onwards.

9 There were still one or two tall chimneys in use into BR days, not always on the locomotives which had carried them originally. For instance, at least one Armstrong Whitworth example, No 45345 was given one in 1949/50.

10 Nos 4826/7/9/30 were converted to oil firing in September 1947 as part of an abortive Government-sponsored scheme, but reverted to coal firing in August 1948. The oil tank in the bunker space of the big 4,000gal tender was not easily seen.

11 Double chimneys on Nos 44765-44767 were replaced by single chimneys during the early 1950s, following comparative tests at Rugby Testing Station in 1950.

12 Electric lighting equipment was removed from Nos 44658 and 44765-67 during the 1950s after falling into disrepair.

13 'Top hat' covers were fitted to the top-feed casings of those boilers

having the later pattern clackboxes — all those with the top-feed in the forward position and some of the earlier boilers with domes.

14 The coal weighing tenders ceased to be used for weighing tests during the 1950s; the steelyards and their casings were removed and the bunkers fixed down. Fire iron tunnels were provided on the right-hand side of the bunker above the relieving gear.

15 Smith-Stone speedometers, with the generator carried on a return crank on the left trailing crankpin, were fitted to a few locomotives beginning in 1961. The original intention was to equip all Class 5s, but this was halted by the Modernisation Plan.

Some reservations are required on the subject of modifications because of the actions of St Rollox works, Glasgow. In a cavalier disregard for official drawings, sloping throatplate boilers with top-feed in either position were fitted more or less indiscriminately at general repairs, regardless of what type the locomotive had been built with, whereas Crewe and Horwich managed to replace like with like. Similarly, top-feed casings of incorrect type were applied as it suited St Rollox, even in LMSR days; at least one domeless boiler was fitted with the narrow casing of a domed boiler, while another domed boiler was given the

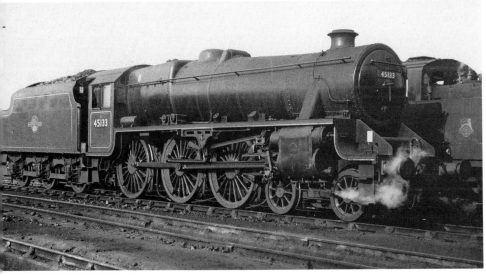

Left:
No 45133 (AW, 5/35) after general repair, on Farnley Junction shed in June 1960. It has a straight throatplate boiler fitted with a dome, and external pipe to the tube cleaner cock. BR lined black livery with 1957 crest and electrification flashes. *G. W. Morrison*

Below:
No 45108 (VF, 5/35) after general repair in the early 1950s, with domed sloping throatplate boiler, barrel/firebox transition over driving axle, no vacuum pump (note fixing for pump arm behind crosshead gudgeon pin), steam sanding. BR lined black livery with 1949 crest. *Ian Allan library*

domeless type of top-feed casing in addition to the dome.

Nor were these oddities confined to boilers. At least one early Class 5, No 45116, was fitted in the early 1950s with new double block brake hangers in place of the original single block type. Modellers seeking accuracy will be well advised to work from photographs of the selected period, for St Rollox was a law unto itself where modifications were concerned!

In addition to the listed modifications there were others applied in small numbers under experimental procedure. Few of these were visible, but as an instance smokebox ash ejector equipment was fitted to four Class 5s (Nos 5334, 5415/35/51) in 1943/44, the distributor for which was mounted high on the left-hand side of the smokebox. It did not last long with the introduction of self-cleaning smokeboxes, also tried out under experimental procedure, eg on No 4825.

Power Classification

Prewar members of the class carried the designation '5P5F' on the cab side above the number, or in some cases where the number had been painted high on the cab side, below it. During World War 2 the simpler designation '5' was used, and this was continued in BR days, appearing below the number.

Livery

Prewar-built examples carried the mixed traffic livery of black, lined out in red, with gold serif characters. The second Armstrong Whitworth order (Nos 5225-5451) was turned out in the 1936 livery variant with sans serif characters on tender, cab side and smokebox number plate, and a very small number of earlier examples received this livery also after repair,

Above:
No 5005 (Crewe, 3/35) in the mid 1940s, running with the wrong type top-feed casing, fitted at St Rollox. LMSR plain black livery with small cabside numbers, power class '5'.
P. Ransome-Wallis

but it was short-lived. During World War 2 any repaints were in unlined black.

The 1946 livery of unlined black with heavy sans serif characters in 'straw' with inset maroon outlines was first applied to No 4768 (Crewe, 4/47) but does not appear to have been used on Horwich-built members of the class.

In BR days the standard mixed traffic livery of black, lined out in red, grey and cream was applied, but before this livery was accepted four

Class 5s were painted early in 1948 in experimental style:

4762	SR green
4763	LNER green
4764	GWR green
45225	LNWR lined black

Withdrawal

The class remained intact until November 1961, when No 45401 was withdrawn after sustaining severe collision damage. In 1962 and 1963 about 20 were scrapped each year, but the flood began in 1964 and in the final year, 1968, no fewer than 151 were withdrawn. The final 46 were taken out of service in August 1968.

Preserved Locomotives

A total of 18 Class 5s have been preserved, including the singleton with Stephenson valve gear. Several have been named by their new owners.

Right:
No 45116 (VF, 6/35) in the early 1950s. Another example of the wrong type top-feed casing fitted at St Rollox, and with double articulated brake blocks (not as-built). BR lined black livery with 1949 crest, power classification '5MT'.
D. Penney

4767	*George Stephenson*	BR mixed traffic lined black, 1957 crest
44806	*Magpie*	BR mixed traffic lined black, 1957 crest
44871	*Sovereign*	BR mixed traffic lined black, 1957 crest
44901	—	—
44932	—	BR mixed traffic lined black, 'British Railways' on tender
5000	—	LMSR black lined red
5025	—	LMSR black lined red
45110	*RAF Biggin Hill*	BR mixed traffic lined black, 1957 crest
45163	—	—
45212	—	BR mixed traffic lined black, 1949 crest
5231	*3rd (Volunteer) Battalion The Worcestershire and Sherwood Foresters Regiment*	—
45293	—	—
45305	*Alderman A. E. Draper*	LMSR black lined red, 1936 style characters
45337	—	—
45379	—	—
45407	—	LMSR black lined red, 1936 style characters
45428	*Eric Treacy*	BR mixed traffic lined black, 1949 crest
45491	—	—

Class 5 - 4-6-0 Caprotti Valve Gear

History

Although these 22 locomotives were built while H. G. Ivatt was CME of the LMSR and London Midland Region of British Railways, they were modifications — albeit substantial ones — of the 'standard' Stanier Class 5, and all the principal dimensions were identical with those of the piston valve version. It is thus appropriate to include them here. The use of poppet valve gear was born of Ivatt's relentless search for ways of reducing costs, increasing availability and eliminating as much depot maintenance as possible. The Caprotti gear, considerably developed since its application to 10 ex-LNWR 'Claughton' rebuilds in 1926-28 and to four ex-GCR 'Lord Faringdon' 4-6-0s shortly afterwards, proved able to increase the mileage between valve examinations from 30-36,000 to 40-48,000 miles. Unfortunately the first 20 locomotives lacked the gutsy pulling power of the piston valve version, and as a result were not popular with enginemen. Modifications to the camboxes used on the last two overcame this and made them very strong, to the point where some enginemen considered them worthy of power class 6.

Features

The 1948 build was in two parts: Nos M4748-44757 had roller bearing axleboxes of Timken manufacture throughout, leading to a coupled wheelbase increase to 7ft 0in+8ft 4in, 4in longer than on previous builds, while Nos 44738-44747 had plain bearings but continued the longer wheelbase. The camboxes of the British Caprotti gear were fixed to the top of the cylinders, between the poppet valve spindles, but the shaft drive to the camboxes from the leading coupled axle was between the frames. The outside steam pipes fed to the front of the cylinders; they were very prominent and cranked just above the

Above:
No M4748 (Crewe, 2/48) at Derby on 20 March 1948, with Timken roller bearings throughout, actuation steam connection from dome, cranked outside steam pipes, open footsteps, and longer sandbox filler pipes already fitted. LMSR plain black livery. *J. M. Jarvis*

cylinders, giving an impression of the arms of a gorilla!

The absence of Walschaerts valve gear allowed the platforms and cab to be redesigned, though the change did nothing for the locomotives' appearance. There was a straight platform at cab floor level behind the cylinders, requiring splashers, with the camboxes standing above it, and a separate front platform at conventional height. These platforms were of lightweight folded construction with no separate valance angles, and the footsteps were of open construction. To give clearance for the cross-drive gearbox beneath the smokebox it was necessary to pitch the boiler 2in higher than on piston valve Class 5s, increasing the height to the chimney top to 12ft 10in. There was no atomiser steam cock on the smokebox side, since the poppet valves needed no atomised oil supply. They did, however, need a steam supply to lift them

on to their seatings when the regulator was open, and this was taken by a covered pipe from the left-hand side of the dome.

The tubular reversing reach rod now extended forward from the cab to the reversing gearbox above the rear of the left-hand cylinder; a cross drive below the front of the boiler led to a similar gearbox on the other side. The two mechanical lubricators on the right-hand running plate were driven from a return crank on the driving crankpin.

Three years later, the last two Caprotti Class 5s were completed, the last of the LMS-type Class 5s to appear. The latest version of the gear incorporated additional exhaust cams

Top right:
No 44743 (Crewe, 6/48) at Newton Heath shed in October 1959 has plain bearing axleboxes throughout, mechanical lubricator drive, straight outside steam pipes, and 'top hat' on top-feed casing. BR lined black livery with 1949 crest. *J. E. Wilkinson*

Right:
No 44756 (Crewe, 6/48) at Nottingham shed about 1961. Timken roller bearings are fitted throughout, and a double chimney. 'SC' smokebox plate has been removed, BR AWS equipped. BR lined black livery with 1957 crest just visible. *J. Wayman*

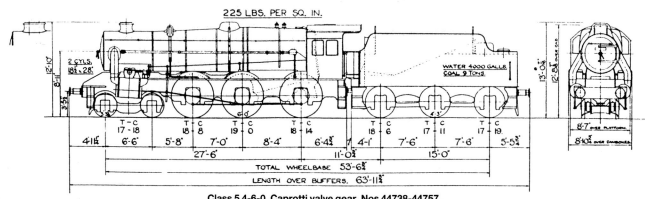

Class 5 4-6-0, Caprotti valve gear, Nos 44738-44757.

to provide variable compression, improving their performance immensely. The camshafts were driven by outside shafts from return cranks on the driving crankpins. Because of this the mechanical lubricators were operated by a return crank on the right-hand trailing crankpin. The cylinder clothing featured a horizontal step just above the centreline, unlike the first 20 locomotives. Straight outside steam pipes were fitted. The revised layout of the Caprotti gear in the cylinder area made it desirable to carry the side platforms very high over the camboxes, thus eliminating

any splashers; they were carried on brackets from the boiler instead of from the frames. SKF roller bearing axleboxes were fitted throughout.

Allocation

The first 20 were sent, five to each depot, to Longsight (Manchester), Llandudno Junction, Bristol and Leeds Holbeck, whence they worked over most of the Midland Division, to Camden on fitted freight trains and on Manchester-North Wales services. The last two were initially allocated to Longsight, and among other duties

frequently worked the 'Pines Express' between Manchester and Birmingham.

Changes during Production

1 The first seven, Nos M4748 (Crewe, 2/48) to 44754 were built with short sandbox filler necks, which brought the filler caps below the reversing reach rod, making filling extremely difficult. Beginning with No 44755 (4/48), therefore, the necks on the left-hand side only were raised to bring the filler caps above the reach

rod, and this was continued in Nos 44738 (Crewe, 6/48) to 44747.

2 Nos 44755 (Crewe, 4/48) to 44757 were built with double chimneys. They were also fitted with electric lighting equipment; the Stone turbo-generator was carried on a bracket low on the right-hand side of the smokebox.

Below:
No 44687 at Birmingham New Street in June 1951. Features include mechanical lubricator drive, and step in cylinder clothing. BR lined black livery with 1949 crest. *A. W. Flowers*

Above:
No 44687 (Horwich, 5/51) at Derby in the early 1950s. This view shows outside drive to the camboxes, reversing shaft from the cab, straight steampipes, connection on the dome for actuation steam, high platform, open footsteps, double chimney, 'SC' plate, and hopper ashpan gear. BR lined black livery with 1949 crest. *P. Ransome-Wallis*

Modifications

1 The short sandbox filler necks on Nos M4748-44754 were replaced very quickly on the left-hand side by long necks.

2 The double chimneys were removed from Nos 44755/7 in the mid-1950s, as was the electric lighting installation.

3 Some, but not all, of the initial 20 were fitted with straight outside steam pipes to the cylinders at general repairs, eg No 44743.

Power Classification

The Caprotti Class 5s always carried the single figure '5' on the cab side. On the first example with 'M' prefix to the LMSR number this was applied below the number; all those with five-figure numbers had the power class above the number.

Livery

Nos 4748-4753 were turned out in plain, unlined black with 'M' prefixes above the cab side numbers and with 'British Railways' in full on the tender sides. Subsequent locomotives carried the normal BR '4' prefix to the number but still with 'British Railways' in full, eg No 44755. At first general repair, and on Nos 44686/87 from new, the BR mixed traffic livery of black, lined red, grey and cream was given, with 1949 and later 1957 crests.

Withdrawal

The first of the original 20 to be condemned was No 44740 in 4/63, and the group became extinct with No 44743 which went in 1/66. The last two Caprotti Class 5s were withdrawn in 10/65 and 1/66 after a life of only 14 years.

Preserved Locomotives

Nil.

LMSR Nos Nil

BR Nos 44686/7
44738-44757

Orders and Construction

Nos	Builder	Lot No	Order No	Building Dates
M4748-44757	Crewe	187	E468	02/48-12/48
44738-44747	Crewe	187	E469	06/48-08/48
44686/87	Horwich	199 (part)	105 (part)	04/51, 05/51

Principal Dimensions

2 Cylinders: 18½in dia × 28in stroke
Coupled Wheels: 6ft 0in
Boiler Pressure: 225lb/sq in
Grate Area: 28.65sq ft
Tractive Effort: 25,455lb

Weight in Working Order:	44738-47	44748-57, 44686/87
Locomotive:	72.2 ton	74.0 ton
Tender:	53.65 ton	53.8 ton
Total:	125.85 ton	127.8 ton

Coal Capacity: 9 ton
Water Capacity: 4,000gal

Class 5XP - Three-Cylinder 4-6-0 'Jubilee'

History

With the ex-LNWR 'Claughton' 4-6-0s proving ever more troublesome and needing to be withdrawn on economic grounds, and with only the two original 'Patriots' in service and a further 15 on order, Stanier found on his arrival at Euston that the locomotive fleet was seriously deficient in reliable second-line express passenger power. He had little alternative but to continue the building of 'Patriots' — with some detail modifications to overcome certain weaknesses – until May 1934, by which time his taper boiler variant of the basic design was ready to go into production. When it did, 191 locomotives of the class were built in two-and-a-half years, 141 in LMSR workshops and 50 from the North British Locomotive Co, Glas-gow. Of the latter, Nos 5557-5581 were built at the Hyde Park works, Springburn (circular builder's plates) and Nos 5582-5606 at the Queens Park works, Polmadie (diamond-shaped plates).

The 'Jubilees' proved probably the most intractable to bring to their full output potential of all Stanier's designs. Their steaming was most unreliable, partly due to defective draughting and partly to unsatisfactory tube proportions, while their efficiency was inferior to that of the 'Patriots' due to the low degree of superheat provided in the earlier builds. This gave rise to many changes in successive production orders and retrospective modifications in earlier examples. When these had been made, it turned the class into very competent performers, though more sensitive to indifferent handling than the Class 5s.

Features

The new 'Jubilees' continued many of the chassis characteristics of the 'Patriots', though visual differences included the valve spindle crosshead guides (mounted on the rear valve chest covers rather than on the motion plates), the cylinder drain cocks (independent of the pressure relief valves, which were fitted on the cylinder covers) and the eccentric rods which were of fluted rather than rectangular section. The bogies were

Below:
Typical duty: No 45561 *Saskatchewan* **(NBL, 6/34) leaves Derby with a West of England express in the early 1950s.** *P. J. Lynch*

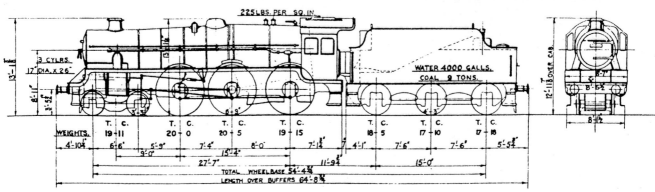

Class 5XP 4-6-0, 3-cylinder 'Jubilee', Nos 5552-5742.

Above:
No 5608 *Gibraltar* **(Crewe, 7/34) at Crewe North shed about 1937. It is fitted with domed sloping throatplate boiler, dry trickle sanding, tall chimney, 6ft 3in wheelbase bogie with plate front stay, and is coupled to a riveted high-sided 3,500gal tender on Fowler 13ft wheelbase chassis. LMSR lined crimson lake livery.** *Photomatic*

re-used from withdrawn 'Claughtons', with modifications, and were of 6ft 3in wheelbase. Dry trickle sanding was provided.

The tapered boiler had a straight throatplate, putting the transition between barrel and Belpaire firebox about 9in behind the intermediate coupled axle. This pattern of boiler (Class 3A) was recognisable also by having five washout plugs on the left-hand side of the firebox (six on the right-hand side). There was no dome, only a small dome-like casing with side bulges over the top-feed equipment. The circular smokebox rested on two separate saddles with a narrow gap between them; the front one was integral with the inside cylinder and the rear one between the outside cylinders. The chimney was fairly tall, with straight parallel sides, and reached 13ft 2¼in above rail. There was a prominent cover, which progressively varied in shape, high on the left-hand side of the smokebox over the atomiser steam cock.

The cab was of Stanier's double side-window pattern with extended roof and fitted with glass hinged windshields on each side. The vacuum brake ejectors were brought to a position just in front of the cab below the handrail, with a long exhaust pipe to the smokebox. A crosshead-driven vacuum pump was also provided. The tender, rather surprisingly, was of Fowler 3,500gal pattern, much narrower than the cab, and with coal rails. A well publicised official photograph of No 5552, issued when

the locomotive was new, showed it coupled to a high straight-sided tender of 3,500gal capacity on Fowler underframe, but this tender, the first of 10, did not enter service until a month later, coupled to No 5607.

Allocation

The 'Jubilees' were always distributed widely to all LMSR Divisions, from Bristol to Glasgow and from Liverpool to Leeds, covering a wide variety of express passenger and fitted freight work. Until the late 1950s no larger passenger class operated on the Midland Division south of Leeds. The depots with the largest allocations were Crewe North, Longsight, Kingmoor and Upperby (Carlisle), Kentish Town, Leeds Holbeck and Newton Heath (Manchester).

Changes during Production

It should be remembered that the original No 5552 (Crewe, 5/34) was renumbered 5642 in April 1935 and the nearly new No 5642 (Crewe, 12/34) became No 5552 *Silver Jubilee,* giving its name to the class (see also the section on livery).

1 The North British-built locomotives, beginning with No 5557 (6/34) introduced the new Stanier 6ft 6in wheelbase side bolster bogie to the class; the side bolsters under the cylinders are not easily seen on most photographs, but the round bar-type front bogie cross-stay is a giveaway as compared with the flat plate stay on the ex-'Claughton' bogies. With the centre pin position unchanged, the wheelbase was increased from 27ft 5½in to 27ft 7in.

2 Nos 5557-5606 all entered service coupled to Stanier 4,000gal tenders of riveted construction.

3 No 5557 also saw the beginning of a complex saga of chimneys, being built with a new design some 2⅜in shorter and of more rounded profile. This reduced the overall height above rail to 12ft 11⅝in. The new design apparently found little favour, because as from No 5564 (8/34) there was a reversion to the taller type.

4 Despite the simultaneous delivery of North British-built locomotives with 6ft 6in wheelbase bogies, Crewe-built Nos 5607-5654 were given 6ft 3in wheelbase ex-'Claughton' bogies.

5 Nos 5607 (Crewe, 6/34) to 5616 entered traffic with a hybrid tender, on the Fowler 13ft wheelbase chassis but with the narrow body continued straight up to greater height and without coal rails; the bunker capacity was nominally unchanged at 5½ ton of coal. These were all built with the taller chimneys.

6 The next 38, Nos 5617 (Crewe,

Below:
No 5573, not yet named *Newfoundland* (NBL, 9/34) when new outside the builder's Hyde Park works, Springburn. Features include the domeless straight throatplate boiler, tall chimney, atomiser steam cock in high position, twin smokebox saddles, pipes to top-feed covered flush in clothing, 6ft 6in wheelbase bogie, vacuum pump with lubricator cup, dry trickle sanding, and hollow axles. It is running with a riveted 4,000gal tender, tender axlebox covers without ribs. Photographic grey simulation of LMSR lined crimson lake livery.
Mitchell Library, Glasgow

Above:
No 5649 *Howard of Effingham* (Crewe, 1/35) at Bedford in April 1936, with 6ft 3in wheelbase bogie and Stanier 3,500gal tender. LMSR lined crimson lake livery. *J. M. Jarvis*

9/34) to 5654 were built with a new Stanier design of 3,500gal tender, similar to the 4,000gal type but on a shorter wheelbase of 13ft and with a bunker holding seven instead of nine ton. It was of riveted construction. This design of tender was not easy to distinguish from its bigger brother, but at the back end the top horizontal row of rivets was about 4in lower from the top of the plating than on the 4,000gal type.

7 The 10 Derby-built examples, starting with No 5655 (12/34) were also outshopped with the shorter chimneys and Stanier 3,500gal tenders.

8 Commencing with No 5665 (Crewe, 11/35) all further 'Jubilees' were built with a modified design of Class 3A boiler having a sloping throatplate but a barrel unaltered in diameter. This brought the transition between barrel and Belpaire firebox slightly in front of the intermediate coupled axle. There was a dome, and the top-feed was given a new design of casing. Two washout inspection doors under small domed covers were provided on each top shoulder of the Belpaire firebox, and there were six washout plugs each side at firebox crown level. The two smokebox saddles were replaced by a single long saddle, integral with the inside cylinder and with vertical ribs. Nos 5665-5694 were built with the

short chimney. Because of the increase in superheater size to 24 elements it was necessary to move the atomiser steam cock to a new position low down on the smokebox side, and no cover was provided.

9 Commencing with No 5695 (Crewe, 3/36) there was a further chimney change. A new one of intermediate height but straight-sided like the original tall chimney was fitted, extending to 13ft 1⅜in above rail. This became the new standard type for the 'Jubilees'.

10 No 5695 also became the first of the class to be fitted with steam sanding instead of dry trickle sanding.

11 The tenders with which these later locomotives were coupled were:

5665/66	Stanier 3,500gal
5667-5694	Stanier 4,000gal
5695-5725,	
5740	Fowler 3,500gal with coal rails (ex-'Royal Scot')
5726-5739,	
5741/42	Stanier 4,000gal

Some of these couplings soon changed, however (see Tender Changes section).

Modifications

1 The first modification began in 1936. In order to provide a pool of spare straight throatplate boilers for exchange at general repairs, 11 'Jubilees' had the frame stretcher in front of the firebox replaced, thereby allowing sloping throatplate boilers to be fitted. They were Nos 5567/90, 5607/8/

10/6/21/2/39/40/57. In practice three of these, Nos 5607/16/22 reverted to straight throatplate boilers in 1938.

2 As the straight throatplate boilers which had been built with the original 14 superheater elements passed through the works at general repairs (108 in number) between 1936 and 1940, they were fitted with the standard larger superheater of 24 elements and with a dome. This left only five domeless boilers, originally fitted to Nos 5642-5646, and these were never fitted with domes; they appeared on a number of 'Jubilees' after exchange at general repairs; their last carriers were Nos 45562 (2/61-11/62), 45586 (2/61-1/65), 45591 (3/60-10/63), 45645 (10/57-10/63) and 45651 (11/60-11/62), in each case immediately prior to withdrawal.

3 In 1937 No 5684 was fitted with a Kylchap double blastpipe and chimney, but it was not entirely satisfactory and was removed in 1938.

4 Nos 5552-5664 were not named when built, but all received nameplates on the leading splashers

Top right:
No 5681 *Aboukir* (Crewe, 1/36) at Crewe North in 1936, with domed sloping throatplate boiler, short chimney, single smokebox saddle, hollow coupled axles, 6ft 6in wheelbase bogie, dry trickle sanding, and riveted 4,000gal tender. LMSR lined crimson lake livery. *Photomatic*

Right:
No 45717 *Dauntless* (Crewe, 7/36) at York South shed about 1949. Steam sanding, Fowler 3,500gal tender (note its narrowness compared with the cab). LMSR black/maroon lined 1946 livery with BR number.
Eric Treacy/Millbrook House collection

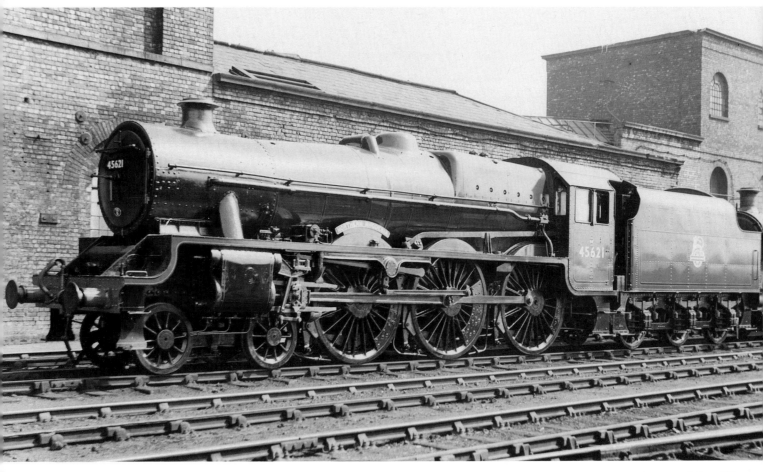

Above:
No 45621 *Northern Rhodesia* (Crewe, 10/34) fresh from general repair, at Crewe works in April 1952. It has emerged fitted with domed sloping throatplate boiler, single smokebox saddle, atomiser steam cock in low position without cover, standard chimney, 6ft 3in wheelbase bogie, no vacuum pump, and with a Stanier 3,500gal tender. BR lined green livery with 1949 crest, power class 6P.
Real Photographs

between January 1936 (when No 5665 was named) and early 1938.

5 Beginning in 1938 the dry trickle sanding on Nos 5552-5694 was replaced by steam sanding.

6 Also beginning in 1938 the crosshead-driven vacuum pumps were removed in order to reduce maintenance costs. The work was completed by 1941.

7 From this time, as renewals of inside cylinders became necessary, the double smokebox saddles gave way to the single long saddles, as provided from No 5665 onwards.

8 Just prior to World War 2 a start was made on fitting BTH speedometers, the generators of which were carried on brackets below the left-hand platform over the trailing wheels. Only a few had been fitted when the war put a stop to the work, and the equipment was not maintained; the brackets long outlasted the speedometers.

9 At about this time rationalisation of the chimneys was put in hand as renewals were needed; a number of interchanges from the original types had already taken place. The intermediate height chimney extending to 13ft 1⅜in above rail was standardised.

10 In 1940 Nos 5553 and 5742 were fitted with double chimneys. The former locomotive only retained it for a short period, but No 5742 ran with it until 1955, when a standard single chimney was fitted.

11 A major rebuilding of Nos 5736 (4/42) and 5735 (5/42) was undertaken, involving fitting the larger Class 2A boiler and double chimney; this raised their power classification from 5XP to 6P. This is detailed in the next chapter.

12 During 1939-41 at least four examples, Nos 5671/98, 5702/08 were fitted with manually-controlled smokebox ash ejector equipment. This was of two types, one operated from a battery of small steam valves low down on the left-hand side of the smokebox, eg No 5698, and the other a large rotary distributor high on the left-hand side of the smokebox, eg No 5671.

13 About 1951 a few 'Jubilees' appeared with chimneys of BR profile, examples being Nos 45561/97, 45608/85. They were subsequently replaced by standard chimneys.

14 In 1958 a double chimney was fitted to No 45596 following tests carried out at Rugby Testing Station with No 45722 in the autumn of 1956. It lasted until the locomotive was withdrawn in July 1966, and is still fitted to the preserved No 45596.

15 In the late 1950s the vertical vacuum pipe from the ejectors to the train pipe under the running plate was replaced by a flexible hose to prevent breakages caused by relative movement of boiler and frames.

16 At about this time the fitting of Smith-Stone speedometers began. The generator was carried on a return crank on the left trailing crankpin. Not all had been fitted when a halt was called to the work with the rundown of steam traction.

17 In the early 1960s, in order to save maintenance and overcome unreliability during steam's dying years, many of the exhaust steam injectors (on the right-hand side) were modified to work on live steam only; the large exhaust steam pipe to the injector was removed and a blank flange fitted to the front of the injector.

Tender Changes

The foregoing account has listed the types of tender with which the 'Jubilees' were first put into traffic. There were very many subsequent changes.

In 1935, at the time of the exchange of identities between Nos 5552 and 5642, the new No 5642 retained its Fowler 3,500gal tender but the new No 5552 and No 5559 exchanged tenders to give No 5552 a Stanier 4,000gal tender and No 5559 a Stanier 3,500gal type.

In 1936 a further 39 Fowler 3,500gal tenders with coal rails were switched from 'Royal Scots' to 'Jubilees' in exchange for their Stanier 4,000gal tenders. The locomotives involved were Nos 5557/60-74/85-99, 5600-06/79.

Between 1937 and 1941 further Stanier 4,000gal tenders were made available as part of an order for 45 Class 4F 0-6-0s, which took Fowler 3,500gal tenders from 'Jubilees'. The 'Jubilees' gaining 4,000gal tenders were 5556/7/60-7/9/70/2/3/85/7/8/90-4/ 6/8/9, 5600-2/4/6-11/4/5/98/9, 5721-4/6/40.

Further random tender changes took place during the early 1940s, as a result of which 'Jubilees' gained the following:

5609/12/3/6, 5726	Fowler 3,500gal with coal rails
5558, 5684	Stanier 3,500gal
5643/5/62, 5703	Stanier 4,000gal

Another major reshuffle took place between 1946 and 1949 to make Stanier 4,000gal tenders available for the 18 'Patriot' rebuilds. The redundant Fowler 3,500gal tenders with coal rails were paired up with Nos 5556/7/61/3/85/7/91/6/8, 5600/11/98, 5721-4/6/40.

Four Stanier 4,000gal tenders bought in 1948 from the War Department (ex-WD Class 8F 2-8-0s) found homes with Nos 45554/85, 45611 and 45725 during 1949 after fitting with steam heating pipes and water pick-up scoops.

After a stable nine years, further large-scale exchanges took place from 1958, this time by taking Stanier 4,000gal tenders from Class 8F 2-8-0s for 41 'Jubilees'; these were Nos 45553/5-7/61/3/8/71/4/86/7/9/91/ 5-8, 45603/5/12/3/5/42/95/8, 45700-2/5/6/8-10/2/7/9/21-3/6/40. They had to be fitted with steam heating pipes.

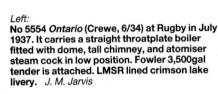

Left:
No 5554 *Ontario* **(Crewe, 6/34) at Rugby in July 1937. It carries a straight throatplate boiler fitted with dome, tall chimney, and atomiser steam cock in low position. Fowler 3,500gal tender is attached. LMSR lined crimson lake livery.** *J. M. Jarvis*

Below:
No 5742 *Connaught* **(Crewe, 12/36) on a Euston-Wolverhampton express on Camden bank about 1947. Visible features are the single smokebox saddlebox and double chimney. Very dirty LMSR lined crimson lake livery.** *Eric Treacy/Millbrook House collection*

Early withdrawals also provided such tenders for Nos 45697 and 45704.

This left 14 'Jubilees' still paired with Fowler 3,500gal tenders with coal rails, namely Nos 45559, 45600/16/79/96, 45707/11/13-6/8/20/4; the Fowler high-sided tenders of 3,500gal capacity had all moved on. But in their final years further juggling took place as a result of which the following gains were made:

45568, 45710/9	Fowler high-sided 3,500gal
45557/75/84/93, 45602/7/15, 45729-31	Stanier 3,500gal

Power Classification

The 'Jubilees' were classed '5XP' by the LMSR, a halfway stage between 5 and 6, and this was applied to the cab sides just below the windows. With the 1946 livery the power class appeared just *below* the number. Under BR's revised all-regions classification they became Class 6P, which appeared just *above* the number.

Livery

All 'Jubilees' were turned out in LMSR crimson lake livery, edged black and lined yellow. Many of the later build from No 5695 received the 1936 sans serif characters from new, but very few of the earlier members of the class were repainted in this style during its short validity.

When No 5642 was renumbered 5552 and named *Silver Jubilee* in April 1935 it was painted in glossy black with chromium plating applied to top-feed casing (which was larger than the current standard and without the side bulges), boiler clothing bands and main steam pipe covers, smokebox door hinges and dart handles, nameplate, cylinder and valve chest covers, handrails, etc. The cab-side numbers and LMS insignia

were in raised cut-out characters, also chromium plated. Only these latter survived the war, the remainder disappearing under paint. In the British Railways era No 45552 received new smaller chromium plated raised numbers on the cab side, with the normal BR crest on the tender.

During World War 2 any of the class requiring a repaint appeared in plain

LMSR Nos 5552-5742

BR Nos 45552-45734
45737-45742

Orders and Construction

Nos	Builder	Lot No	Order No	Building Dates
5552-5556	Crewe	97	E381	05/34-06/34
5557-5606	North British	118	–	06/34-04/35
5607-5636	Crewe	112	E388	06/34-12/34
5637-5654	Crewe	112	E389	12/34-02/35
5655-5664	Derby	113	8610	12/34-01/35
5665-5694	Crewe	121	E396	11/35-03/36
5695-5724	Crewe	129	E398	03/36-09/36
5725-5742	Crewe	129	E399	09/36-12/36

Principal Dimensions

3 Cylinders: 17in dia × 26in stroke
Coupled Wheels: 6ft 9in
Boiler Pressure: 225lb/sq in
Grate Area: 29.5sq ft (5552-5664)
            31.0sq ft (remainder)
Tractive Effort: 26,610lb

Weight in Working Order:
  Locomotive: 77.35 ton to 79.55 ton
  Tender: 42.7 ton to 53.65 ton
  Total: 120.05 ton to 133.20 ton
Coal Capacity: 5.5 to 9 ton
Water Capacity: 3,500 to 4,000gal

Above:
No 45561 *Saskatchewan* **at Cricklewood shed in July 1963, with a straight throatplate boiler with dome, 'top hat' on top-feed casing, and flexible vertical vacuum pipe below ejectors. It is not fitted with BR AWS. It is seen 14 months before withdrawal. BR lined green livery with 1957 crest and electrification flashes.**
R. A. Panting

unlined black, though a few managed to retain a careworn crimson colour throughout. Before the adoption of the 1946 livery, No 5573 appeared for a short while in blue-grey with broad maroon edging, and No 5594 was fully repainted in LMSR crimson lake with most of the prewar lining. A significant number received the 1946 livery of black with broad maroon edging and straw lining, this practice continuing (with 'British Railways' lettering and five-figure numbers, after a brief spell of using an 'M' number prefix) into BR days. Early in 1948 No 45604 was repainted in a light green shade with red and grey lining and 'British Railways' tender lettering. But later that year the decision was taken to paint passenger classes such as the 'Jubilees' GWR dark green with orange and black lining (including clothing bands on the boiler barrel but not the firebox) with the appropriate crest on the tender.

In the final years any full repaints were done in unlined dark green. From September 1964 remaining examples received a broad yellow diagonal stripe on each cab panel to indicate that they were not allowed to work under the 25kV overhead wires south of Crewe.

Withdrawal

The first withdrawal was involuntary; No 45637 was so badly wrecked in the Harrow multiple collision on 8 October 1952 that it was officially withdrawn in December 1952. Thereafter the class remained intact until No 45609 was condemned in September 1960, and only three (Nos 45616/9/30) were scrapped in 1961. But thereafter they were withdrawn rapidly, the last to go being No 45562 in November 1967.

Preserved Locomotives

Four of the class have been preserved:
- 5593 *Kolhapur*
  Straight throatplate – LMSR lined red
- 45596 *Bahamas*
  Straight throatplate and double chimney – BR lined green
- 5690 *Leander*
  Sloping throatplate – LMSR lined red
- 45699 *Galatea*
  Sloping throatplate – Not yet restored, spares for *Leander*

Left:
No 5579 *Punjab* **(NBL, 10/34) about 1946. The wrong type of top-feed cover has been fitted at St Rollox, and a short chimney is carried. LMSR wartime unlined black livery.**
P. Ransome-Wallis

Class 6P - Three-Cylinder 4-6-0 Rebuilt 'Jubilee' and Rebuilt 'Patriot'

The inclusion of rebuilt 'Patriots' as Stanier locomotives may be regarded as controversial, since the first was not 'rebuilt' until almost four years after Stanier's secondment on Government service and two years after Fairburn had been confirmed as CME. Nevertheless, as they were almost entirely new locomotives which closely followed the design of the two 'Jubilees' rebuilt under Stanier's direction, it is thought reasonable to describe them here.

History

By the start of World War 2 the 'Royal Scot' 4-6-0s were beginning to show their age; it was apparent that major alterations would be needed to restore their reliability and availability. In particular their frames were very troublesome with fractures, and the smokebox could not be kept airtight for long periods. Their weight did not allow their use on the Midland Division, where the 'Jubilees' were regularly overloaded. The one-off No 6170 *British Legion* with Class 2 boiler pointed the way forward, but this boiler did not have ideal pro-

portions and steaming was not perfect, while it looked — and was — distinctly heavy at the front end. A revised boiler was therefore designed, shorter in the barrel but using the same Belpaire firebox, and a vehicle for testing it was sought. Under the difficult conditions of wartime, when it was necessary to reuse as much existing material as possible, it was decided to rebuild two modern 'Jubilees' with this Class 2A boiler, and this was done under experimental procedure. The good reports of these two locomotives in heavy wartime traffic between Leeds and Glasgow led to authority being given for an even more comprehensive rebuild of the 'Royal Scots'.

An appraisal of the likely needs for large express power in the postwar world identified a need for a total of 91 locomotives in power class 6P. There would be 71 'Royal Scots' and the two rebuilt 'Jubilees', leaving a need for 18 more. It was felt that the greater advantage lay in drastically rebuilding 'Patriots' to bring them into line with Nos 5735/36, rather than rebuilding more 'Jubilees'. It is remarkable that this 1944 appraisal of

postwar needs should have been so blinkered as to fail to foresee the scale of the need. Within seven years the LM Region was staking a claim for 10 BR Standard 'Britannias' in this power range; even when these were delivered, no large 4-6-0s became available to the Midland Division south of Leeds until mid-1957.

Features

The Class 2A boiler used on Nos 5735/36 was some 15in shorter in the barrel than that on No 6170, and the two were not interchangeable. The top-feed was moved forward to the front (parallel) ring of the barrel and given a more slender casing with straight top. Retaining the original inside cylinder with its integral smokebox saddle designed to carry the smaller 'Jubilee' Class 3A boiler made it necessary to pitch the new boiler 4in higher above rail and provide a tapered adapter plate to the curved surface of the saddle, giving it a rather clumsy appearance. A double chimney was fitted. New brake hangers with articulated twin brake blocks were provided.

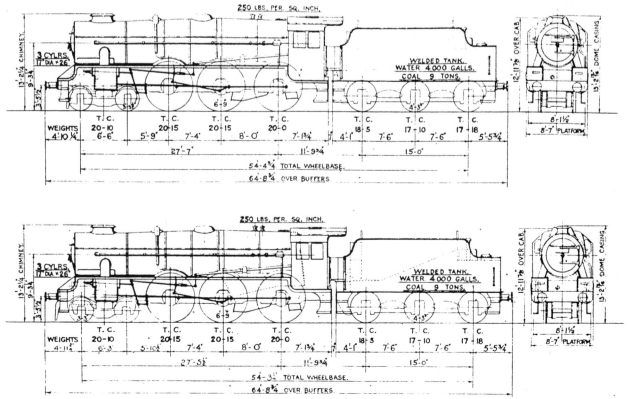

Class 6P 4-6-0, 3-cylinder rebuilt 'Jubilee', Nos 5735/6.
Class 6P 4-6-0, 3-cylinder rebuilt 'Patriot', Nos 5514-5540.

Above:
No 5736 *Phoenix* (reb 5/42), as newly converted.
Visible features are the straight top to the
top-feed casing, atomiser steam cock in high
position, new straight reversing reach rod,
single smokebox saddle with thick packing
plate, twin articulated brake blocks, and BTH
speedometer. Photographic grey simulation of
LMSR lined crimson lake livery. *Ian Allan library*

Right:
No 45736 *Phoenix* on Newton Heath shed in
1958. It now has a top-feed casing with curved
top, smoke deflectors, BR AWS, flexible hose
for vertical vacuum pipe below ejectors, and no
speedometer. BR lined green livery with 1957
crest. *J. E. Wilkinson*

Top right:
Unrebuilt Patriot No 5523, unnamed, on Edge
Hill shed in the 1930s.
Eric Treacy/Millbrook House collection

The existing cab and 4,000gal
tender were retained. Due to the
larger boiler it was necessary to fit a
new straight reversing reach rod from
the cab, outside the intermediate
splasher, with a modified steady
bracket to support it.

The rebuilding of the 'Patriots' was
on very similar lines, but involved not
only the new boiler but also new
frames, cylinders, cabs and tenders,
the later transferred from 'Jubilees'.
The first 12 'Patriots', Nos 5500-5511
incorporated too much material from
their LNWR 'Claughton' ancestors to
be suitable for rebuilding, but from
the remainder the wheels, bogie,
motion and other components could be
used. New 17in diameter cylinders
were fitted, with the saddle element
correctly radiused for the smokebox of

the Class 2A boiler. The visible differences from Nos 5735/36 were mainly:

(i) Flat rectangular section eccentric rods (ex-'Patriot')
(ii) 6ft 3in wheelbase bogie
(iii) Rocking grate and hopper ashpan, the hopper door operating gear projecting on the left-hand side between intermediate and trailing coupled wheels
(iv) Double side-window cab with leading cab side windows fixed and flat beading round window openings.

All were ultimately named, the last (No 5528, rebuilt 8/47) as late as 1960. Remarkably, perhaps, eight of the names came from 'Claughtons' and survived two rebuildings!

Allocation

Nos 5735/36 were sent first to Leeds Holbeck for working Leeds-Glasgow expresses via the Settle & Carlisle and G&SWR routes, where they outshone the 'Jubilees' on the heavy wartime loads. Subsequently they were transferred to the Western Division in the general pool with rebuilt 'Royal Scots'.

Below:
No 5530 *Sir Frank Ree* (reb 10/46) in new condition ex-works, with straight-topped top-feed casing, original valve gear with rectangular section eccentric rod, built-up valve spindle crosshead guides on valve chest cover, twin articulated brake blocks, hopper ashpan operating gear, and welded 4,000gal tender. LMSR black/maroon lined 1946 livery.
Ian Allan library

All the 'Patriot' rebuilds were initially allocated to such Western Division depots as Camden, Crewe North, Edge Hill (Liverpool) and Carlisle Upperby, working turn and turn about with rebuilt 'Royal Scots'. In their last years they wandered much more widely.

Changes during Production

None of a visual nature.

Below:
No 45531 *Sir Frederick Harrison* (reb 11/47) at Derby in May 1948 carrying a special livery of LNER apple green with LNWR lining.
J. M. Jarvis

Modifications

1 Commencing in 1950 all 22 locomotives were fitted with the short curved smoke deflectors alongside the smokebox as applied to the rebuilt 'Royal Scots' also.
2 At about this time the top-feed casings were altered to a pattern with a curved top.
3 In the late 1950s all were fitted with Smith-Stone speedometers, the generator for which was fitted on a return crank on the left-hand trailing crank pin.
4 Also at this late period the vertical vacuum pipe from the ejectors to the train pipe below the platform was replaced by a flexible hose to eliminate breakages.

Power Classification

When Nos 5735/36 were rebuilt the power classification was not altered from the previous 5XP. After a few months they were uprated to 6P, and all the 'Patriot' rebuilds were so classed from the start. From 1951 this became 7P on the BR scale

Livery

Nos 5735/36 were turned out in plain wartime black, despite official photographs showing No 5736 in photographic grey simulation of LMSR crimson lake lined livery.

'Patriots' rebuilt before 1948, eight in number, were put into traffic in the LMSR 1946 passenger livery of black, with the platform valances (except under the cab) and the edges of the cab and tender sides carrying a broad maroon stripe edged straw. The cylinder clothing bands, the front and rear boiler barrel clothing bands and the rear firebox clothing angle at the cab had a narrower maroon stripe similarly edged. Heavy sans serif characters were used. No 45531 was turned out early in 1948 in an experimental livery of LNER apple green with LNWR red, grey and cream lining and with 'British Railways' on the tender, but this was not perpetuated.

One or two were painted in the black BR livery, lined red, grey and cream as applied to second-line passenger classes, but eventually all were finished in BR green (the GWR shade) with orange and black lining. From September 1964 the few survivors received a broad diagonal yellow stripe on each cab side panel to show that they were barred from working under the 25kV overhead wires south of Crewe.

LMSR Nos 5514/21/6/8-32/40, 5735/6

Rebuilding

Nos	Rebuilding Dates
5735/6	05/42, 04/42
5521/30	10/46
5514/26/8/9/31/40	02/47-11/47
45512/23/5/7/32/4-6/45	05/48-12/48
45522	02/49

Not turned out in this order.
All rebuilding was carried out at Crewe.

Principal dimensions

3 Cylinders:	17in dia× 26in stroke
Coupled Wheels:	6ft 9in
Boiler Pressure:	250lb/sq in
Grate Area:	31.25sq ft
Tractive Effort:	29,590lb

Withdrawal

The first to be withdrawn was No 45514 in May 1961. No others went until No 45536 in December 1962, after which withdrawals were rapid and completed with No 45530, the first rebuild, in December 1965. Nos 45735/36 were withdrawn in October and September 1964 respectively.

Preserved Locomotives

Nil.

BR Nos 45512/4/21-3/5-32/4-6/40/5*, 45735/6
*Construction continued by British Railways

Weight in Working Order:	
Locomotive:	82.0 ton
Tender:	53.65 ton
Total:	135.65 ton
Coal Capacity:	9 ton
Water Capacity:	4,000gal

Below:
No 45522 *Prestatyn* (reb 2/49) at Kentish Town shed about 1959 with top-feed casing with curved top, smoke deflectors, BR AWS, and flexible hose for vertical vacuum pipe below ejectors. BR lined green livery with 1957 crest.
J. Davenport

Class 6P - Three-Cylinder 4-6-0 Rebuilt 'Royal Scot'

These locomotives are included because, although the first rebuild was not completed until just after Stanier's secondment to Government service, all the design work was completed under his direction and to his standards.

History

The problems besetting the 70 parallel boiler 'Royal Scot' 4-6-0s built in 1927 and 1930 have been touched on in the last chapter: frame fractures, smokebox leakage and, by 1942, boilers already 15 years old after bearing the brunt of much heavy express passenger service in which they were worked very hard. At this time there were only 37 Pacifics, plus the rather unreliable turbine-driven No 6202. Having proved the Class 2A boiler on the two 'Jubilee' rebuilds, Stanier could confidently go to the Mechanical & Electrical Engineering Committee of the LMSR for financial sanction to rebuild the entire class with the same type of boiler and a much improved front end. Approval in December 1942, despite the difficult wartime conditions, allowed the first rebuilt locomotive to be put into service seven months later. The 1935 rebuild No 6170 from the experimental high-pressure locomotive No 6399 was the starting point for the redesign.

The work took almost 12 years to complete, by which time some of the original parallel boilers were 28 years old, though in 1947 and 1948 — when only seven were rebuilt — priority was being given to the rebuilding of 'Patriots'. The work not only enhanced the performance of the 'Royal Scots' but also gave them a new lease of life, in some cases of 20 years or more.

Features

The Class 2A boiler was interchangeable with that used on the two 'Jubilee' and the 18 'Patriot' rebuilds. Below the platform new cylinders were fitted, having much more extended valve chests. The original coupling rods, with their split brasses in square ends for the leading crankpin, were reused, as were the connecting rods, cross-heads and valve gear. The valve spindle crosshead guides, which on the parallel boiler locomotives were carried on an outrigger from the motion plate, were transferred to the rear valve chest covers and the outriggers cut back. The new frames were deeper and rounded at the front buffer beam, with the lifting holes visible. The cover between the frames below the smokebox was higher than on the 'Jubilee' and 'Patriot' rebuilds, and featured two footsteps. A double chimney was fitted. The original single side-window cab was retained.

Allocation

The first few rebuilds were allocated to Leeds Holbeck shed for working Leeds-Glasgow trains, and were the only 'Royal Scots' to work on the Midland Division until 1957. The remainder went to Western Division depots and to Polmadie for West Coast main line work. The principal depots involved were Camden, Crewe North, Edge Hill (Liverpool), Longsight (Manchester), Carlisle Upperby and Polmadie.

Changes during Production

1 Only No 6103 (6/43) was fitted with a BTH speedometer, its generator carried on a bracket over the left trailing coupled wheel; under wartime conditions it was omitted from all subsequent rebuilds.

2 No 6119 when rebuilt (9/44) was given plain rectangular section coupling rods with circular bushed ends

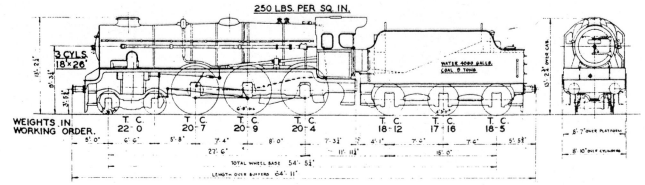

Class 6P 4-6-0, 3-cylinder rebuilt 'Royal Scot', Nos 6100-6169.

for the leading crankpins. No 6160 (2/45) also received this type of rods and a few others may also have done so.

3 When No 6104 was rebuilt in March 1946 it ran for some time coupled to a Stanier 3,500gal tender.

4 Commencing with No 6139 (11/46) all further rebuilds were fitted with rocking grates and hopper ashpans to facilitate servicing. The operating gear for the ashpan hopper doors

projected on the left-hand side immediately behind the intermediate coupled wheel below the coupling rod.

5 A minor detail from about this time is that the valve spindle crosshead guides, hitherto of cast non-ferrous metal, were changed on further rebuilds to a fabricated design of flat guides with bobbin spacers.

6 From about 1947 all original coupling rods with square ends and split brasses to the leading crankpins were replaced at rebuilding by new fluted rods with circular bushed ends.

7 Also from that year all rebuilds were provided with large rectangular sandboxes on the running plate

between the intermediate and trailing coupled wheels, to counter cases of bent coupling rods as a result of high-speed slipping. Sandpipes from them fed to the back of the intermedi-

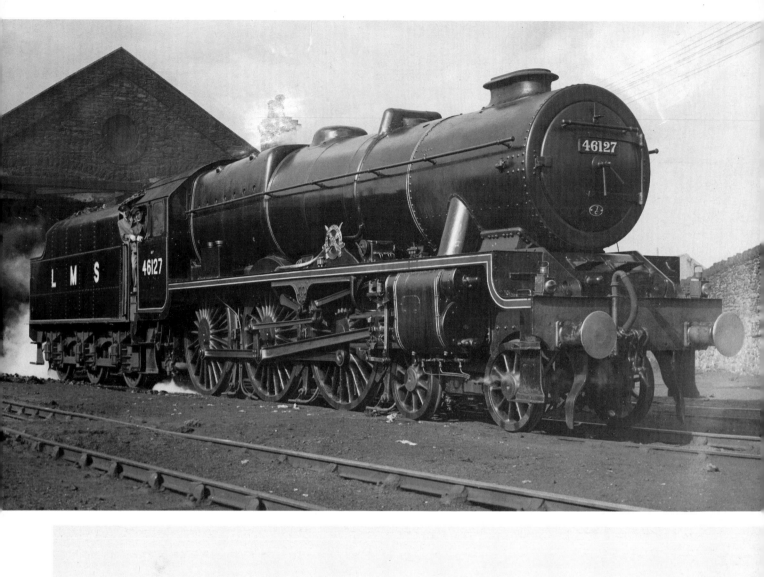

ate wheels and the front of the trailing wheels.

8 On rebuilding in October 1946 No 6161 was fitted experimentally with a self-cleaning smokebox; it is not known whether there was any form of external marking. Its development period to full effectiveness proved difficult and lengthy and after a few years it was abandoned.

9 No 6115 (8/47) was fitted with short curved smoke deflectors for trial. They were judged satisfactory and all subsequent rebuilds from 1949 were fitted new.

Modifications

1 Rear sandboxes were retrospectively fitted to all rebuilds in the late 1940s at works overhauls.

2 Smoke deflectors of the pattern applied to No 6115 were fitted to all

earlier rebuilds from 1949 (but see item **4** below).

3 In the early 1950s the straight-topped top-feed casing began to give way to a revised type with curved top.

LMSR Nos 6101/3/4/8/9/11/2/4-22/4-33/5/8/9/44-7/9/50/2/7/9/61/6/8/9

Rebuilding

Nos	*Rebuilding Dates*
6103/8/9/12/7/24/5/32/46†	06/43-12/43
6116/9/20/7/9/31/3/8/45†	01/44-12/44
6101/22/6/44/9/50/2/9/60/6/9†	01/45-12/45
6104/14/8/21/8/39/47/57/61/8†	01/46-12/46
6111/5/35†	01/47-10/47
46105/54/62/7†	01/48-12/48
46102/6/23/30/43/53†	05/49-12/49
46100/7/13/36/41/55†	03/50-12/50
46142/64	02/51, 06/51
46140/58/65†	05/52-09/52
46110/34/51/63†	01/53-12/53
46148/56	07/54, 05/54
46137	03/55
†Not in this order	

Principal Dimensions

3 Cylinders: 18in dia × 26in stroke
Coupled Wheels: 6ft 9in
Boiler Pressure: 250lb/sq in
Grate Area: 31.25sq ft
Tractive Effort: 33,150lb

4 In 1954 No 46106 was fitted with smoke deflectors of a similar pattern to those on the BR Standard 4-6-2s. These were longer than those on other 'Royal Scots', flat but slightly curved-

BR Nos 46100-46169*
*Rebuilding continued by BR

Weight in Working Order:
  Locomotive: 83.0 ton
  Tender: 54.65 ton
  Total: 137.65 ton
Coal Capacity: 9 ton
Water Capacity: 4,000gal

in at the top, and with a continuous handrail inset from the top and front edges. No other members of the class were modified in this way.

5 In the late 1950s Smith-Stone speedometers were fitted to most 'Royal Scots'; the generator was mounted as usual on a return crank on the left trailing crankpin.

6 Also about this time the vertical vacuum pipe from the ejectors to the train pipe below the running plate was changed to a flexible hose to prevent breakage due to relative movement of boiler and frames.

Power Classification

Under the LMSR the rebuilt 'Royal Scots' were unchanged from the original version at 6P. From 1951 under the BR classification they became Class 7P.

Livery

With the first 30 or so rebuilds being carried out under wartime conditions, these were originally turned out in plain unlined black with LMSR serif characters. A number receiving general repairs or after rebuilding in 1946 and 1947 appeared in the 1946 LMSR livery of black with broad maroon bands edged in straw.

Under BR auspices a few 'Royal Scots' were turned out from Crewe in black with LNWR lining of red, cream and grey with 'British Railways' on the tender, but these were soon overtaken by the standard livery of dark green lined orange and black, with the current crest on the tender and the power class above the number on the cab side. Cylinders and smoke deflectors were invariably black.

From September 1964 the few survivors had a broad yellow diagonal stripe painted on each cab panel to indicate that they were not allowed to work under the 25kV overhead wires south of Crewe.

Withdrawal

The first to be withdrawn were Nos 46100/39 in October 1962, but the remainder of that year saw a further 27 taken out of service. The last to go was No 46115 in December 1965.

Preserved Locomotives

Two 'Royal Scots' live on:

6100 *Royal Scot*
at Bressingham in LMSR crimson livery (which, since it was not rebuilt until 6/50, it never carried while in this form).

6115 *Scots Guardsman*
at Tyseley in LMSR 1946 black livery with maroon edges, which is authentic for this locomotive.

Left:
No 46119 *Lancashire Fusilier* (reb 9/44) at Camden in the early 1950s. It is running with new rectangular section coupling rods, and smoke deflectors. BR lined green livery with 1949 crest. *Ian Allan library*

Below left:
No 46110 *Grenadier Guardsman* (reb 1/53) on Camden shed in 1964. It has the curved top to top-feed casing, hopper ashpan operating gear, BR AWS, Smith-Stone speedometer, and flexible hose on the vertical vacuum pipe below the ejectors. BR lined green livery (very dirty) with 1957 crest and electrification flashes. *N. Gascoine*

Below:
No 46100 *Royal Scot* (reb 6/50) newly converted. Features to note are the special nameplate commemorating US tour in 1933, and the short rain gutter on the cab roof. BR lined green livery with 1949 crest. *BR LM Region*

Bottom:
No 46106 *Gordon Highlander* (reb 9/49) on Longsight shed in April 1959 carrying BR-pattern smoke deflectors. *Photomatic*

Class 6P - Three-Cylinder 4-6-0
British Legion

History

In 1929 the North British Locomotive Co built an experimental super-pressure locomotive for the LMSR, based on the 'Royal Scots' which the firm had built two years earlier, but modified as a three-cylinder compound, carrying a Schmidt three-pressure water-tube boiler working at 1,400-1,800, 900 and 250lb/sq in. The locomotive was never taken into LMSR stock; when less than two months old, while on trial, one of the super-pressure tubes burst, killing a man in the cab. After this No 6399 was laid up

Below:
No 6170 *British Legion* (reb 11/35) newly converted, carrying the No 2 boiler with top-feed near dome, with inclined main steam pipes, cylinders with extended valve chests, valve spindle crosshead guides on valve chest covers, original valve gear, fluted coupling rods with square split brasses for leading crank pin, vacuum pump, double side-window cab, and attached to a riveted 4,000gal tender. LMSR lined crimson lake livery. *Ian Allan library*

in Derby works, whence it ran one or two desultory trials only. In 1935 Stanier took the locomotive in hand and completely rebuilt it as a new and improved 'Royal Scot'. The chassis was reused with modifications and a new conventional boiler fitted (Class 2). In this form it became the precursor for the subsequent rebuilding of the 'Royal Scots'.

Features

The original frames were retained. New cylinders were fitted, with extended valve chests, and the valve spindle crosshead guides were moved on to the rear steam chest covers. The existing coupling and connecting rods and Walschaerts valve gear were reused. A new side bolster bogie of 6ft 6in wheelbase was fitted. A new double side-window cab was provided, and the vacuum ejectors moved to Stanier's usual position just in front of it, with long exhaust pipe to the

smokebox. The vacuum pump was retained.

The principal change lay in the new tapered boiler which, in the event, was to be unique to No 6170. It had a gently curved Belpaire firebox, dome and adjacent top-feed. The barrel was some 1ft 3in longer than that of the later Class 2A boiler developed from it, giving a rather front-heavy, forward-leaning look which was accentuated by the inclined outside main steam-pipes. The cylindrical smokebox rested on a fabricated saddle which was independent of the inside cylinder, and a shapely single chimney was fitted. The locomotive was coupled to a Stanier 4,000gal tender transferred from a 'Jubilee' order.

Even when other changes were made retrospectively to bring No 6170 into line with the 'Royal Scot' rebuilds proper, it was always distinguishable from them (and from the 'Jubilee' and 'Patriot' rebuilds) by the unique combination of double side-window cab and the boiler with dome and top-feed close together.

Allocation

The initial allocation was to Longsight (Manchester) depot, where *British Legion* put up excellent performances on services to and from Euston. Later it was pooled with other rebuilt 'Royal Scots' on the Western Division, usually at Crewe North or Camden, though it always had a slightly more restricted route availability than the other rebuilt 4-6-0s.

Modifications

1 At first steaming was a little erratic, and changes were made to the draughting and to the tube layout. The only visual effect of this was that the steampipe casings to the outside

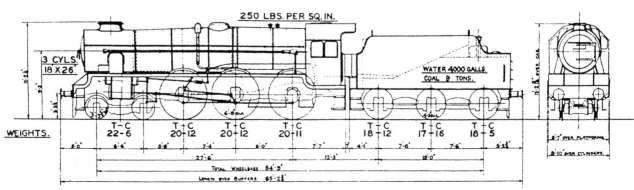

Class 6P 4-6-0, 3-cylinder *British Legion*, No 6170.

cylinders were made vertical but somewhat wider.

2 In 1938 the vacuum pump was removed.

3 About 1946 the locomotive was fitted with a double chimney standard with the other rebuilt 'Royal Scots'.

4 At the same time the atomiser steam cock, which had been placed high on the smokebox side under a slender pear-shaped cover was moved down to a position just above the handrail under a revised cover.

5 Around 1949 standard curved smoke deflectors were fitted.

6 In the late 1950s a Smith-Stone speedometer was fitted, with the generator on a return crank on the left trailing crankpin.

7 At about this time also the top-feed casing, which was of the more common Stanier type having a straight top centre section with separate side covers, acquired a 'top hat' addition.

No 6170 was never fitted with the additional rear sandboxes on the side platforms.

Power Classification

The 6P classification on the LMSR was applied below the cab windows. In 1951 this became 7P under the BR system; it appeared above the numbers on the cab side.

Livery

As rebuilt No 6170 received the standard LMSR crimson lake livery with yellow lining and black edges. It is not known whether it was painted unlined black during wartime, but this is probable. It certainly gained LMSR 1946 black livery with maroon stripes edged straw, and was still so painted when in 1948 it received its BR number and 'British Railways' on the tender. Subsequently it received the standard BR dark green livery with orange and black lining and crest on the tender.

Withdrawal

British Legion was withdrawn in December 1962 and was not preserved.

LMSR No 6170

BR No 46170

Rebuilding

Built as No 6399 *Fury* in December 1929, it was rebuilt at Crewe in November 1935 as No 6170 *British Legion*.

Principal Dimensions

3 Cylinders: 18in dia × 26in stroke
Coupled Wheels: 6ft 9in
Boiler Pressure: 250lb/sq in
Grate Area: 31.25sq ft
Tractive Effort: 33,150lb

Weight in Working Order:
  Locomotive: 84.05 ton
  Tender: 54.65 ton
  Total: 138.70 ton

Class 7P - Four-Cylinder 4-6-2 'Princess'

History

The operating demand facing Stanier in his first year at Euston was for a new heavy express passenger locomotive capable of working 500-ton trains throughout the 401 miles between Euston and Glasgow, including the severe climbs to Grayrigg, Shap Summit and Beattock Summit. Clearly this would require a big boiler with wide firebox to give ample grate area, and correspondingly large ashpan, which in turn made a trailing truck necessary. The answer had therefore to be a 4-6-2. Stanier decided that the design could be based on the GWR 'King' with which he was familiar, though including some elements from recent LMSR practice. The first two members of the class incorporated his ideas on Swindon-style low superheat and other features.

The two-year period while they were evaluated on Anglo-Scottish services showed up problem areas, both in the boiler and in the tender, which was unable to feed coal satisfactorily to the fireman on long runs; these problems were in large measure rectified in the remaining 10 locomotives when built. The 'Princesses' remained in front-line express passenger service for over 25 years until made redundant by dieselisation.

Features

The rear-end frames under the firebox were of splayed sandwich construction, partly masking the trailing truck. The leading bogie, with a wheelbase of no less than 7ft 6in, was of bar frame form and carried its load through prominent side bolsters. The outside cylinders were placed over the trailing bogie axle as in GWR four-cylinder classes, while the inside cylinders were placed well forward to drive the leading coupled axle, providing a sizeable platform under the smokebox door. The outside steam pipes to the cylinders had to be S-shaped, another Swindon trait. Yet another was the long open-jawed outside slidebars with a tiebar between them, supported by an open-fronted motion plate between leading and intermediate coupled wheels. Below them on the left-hand side was a crosshead-driven vacuum pump. The outside Walschaerts valve gear was unusual in that the eccentric rod was coupled to the *outside* of the expansion link part way up rather than to a tail, an arrangement previously only used on inside applications of the gear. The axles were solid.

Dry trickle sanding was provided; this was to be a reinstated feature of LMSR practice for about three years. Two mechanical lubricators were fitted, a large 16-feed cylinder lubricator on the left-hand platform and a 10-feed axlebox lubricator on the other side.

The boiler with its Belpaire wide firebox was very long; the sloping throatplate of the firebox put the transition between boiler barrel and firebox about 1ft 6in behind the trailing coupled axle. There were seven washout plugs on each firebox flank at crown level, but no washout inspection doors on the shoulders. There was no dome, only a top-feed under a small dome-like cover with side bulges; the feed pipes to it were outside the boiler clothing under covers. There were four squat pop safety valves in square formation on the firebox top along

Right:
Typical duty: No 46209 *Princess Beatrice* (Crewe, 8/35) at grips with the 1 in 75 of Shap bank on the morning Birmingham-Glasgow & Edinburgh express approaching Scout Green box about 1949.
Eric Treacy/Millbrook House collection

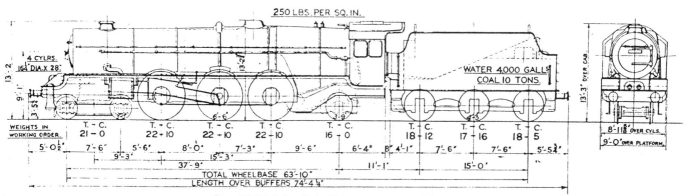

Class 7P 4-6-2, 4-cylinder 'Princess', Nos 6200/1/3-12.

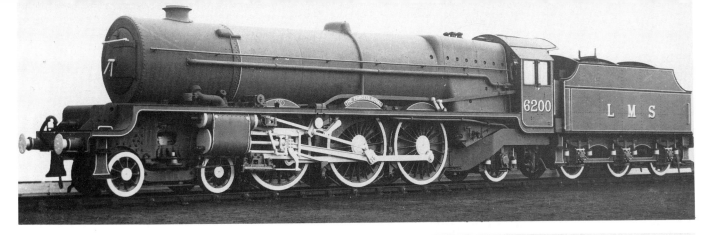

with the Caledonian-pattern hooter mounted horizontally. A blow-off cock was fitted at foundation ring level on the left-hand side of the firebox near the front.

A rather stern-looking double side-window cab was provided, with a hinged glass draught screen on the driver's side only. There was no footstep below the cab; this would have been impracticable due to the throw-over on curves. The reversing reach rod was in two sections, meeting at a short cross-shaft behind the left trailing splasher. The single vacuum ejector was mounted in front of the cab with a long exhaust pipe to the smokebox.

A new design of tender was used. The tank and bunker were reminiscent of the Fowler 3,500gal tender, but were of full cab width and with no coal rails. The underframe had a 15ft wheelbase and roller bearing axleboxes, identifiable by their double circular covers.

Allocation

The first two members of the class were allocated to Camden shed for Anglo-Scottish workings. From the late 1930s they and their 10 sisters took second place to the 'Duchess' Pacifics, and were variously based at Camden, Crewe North, Edge Hill and Polmadie.

Changes during Production

The locomotives built in 1935, Nos 6203 (Crewe, 7/35) to 6212 introduced significant changes.

1 The boiler was redesigned to provide a larger superheater and a combustion chamber in the firebox; this brought the boiler barrel/firebox transition forward to a point marginally in front of the trailing coupled axle. There were now eight washout plugs on each flank of the firebox at crown level, and in addition there were two washout inspection doors, under domed covers, on each firebox shoulder. The new boilers were still without domes. The feed pipes to the top-feed were now inset flush in the boiler clothing. No blow-off cocks were fitted on the firebox.

2 The atomiser steam cock, previously high on the left-hand side of the smokebox and with a prominent cover, was moved to a position below the ejector exhaust pipe and left uncovered. Its place was taken by a small cock controlling lubrication to the regulator in the superheater header.

3 The motion and valve gear showed several changes. Shorter slidebars were used, supported by an 'external' motion plate a little further forward. New expansion links with offset bottom tails of conventional type were fitted, and the eccentric rods had large ball bearing ends to the return cranks, with circular brass covers.

4 All locomotive axles were bored hollow.

5 The reversing reach rod was still in two sections, but the short intermediate cross-shaft was moved to the front of the trailing splasher, with a steady bracket on the firebox side for the rear section.

6 Three mechanical lubricators were provided; the 12-feed cylinder lubricator remained on the left-hand side, but there were now 12-feed and eight-feed lubricators before and behind the leading splasher on the right-hand side.

7 The chimney was given a slightly more rounded, softer line.
8 Hinged glass draught screens were fitted on both sides of the cab.
9 The locomotives were coupled to standard 9-ton 4,000gal tenders of riveted construction.

Modifications

In view of their leading role on heavy express work, modifications started quite early in the lives of the 'Princesses'.

1 For a very brief period at the end of 1933 No 6201 ran with a fabricated double chimney of stovepipe type and unbecoming looks.

2 By 1934 Nos 6200/01 had been fitted with hinged glass draught screens on the fireman's side also.

3 In 1935 the tenders on Nos 6200/01 were replaced by standard 9-ton 4,000gal tenders to overcome coal feed problems on long runs.

4 In November 1935 No 6201 appeared with an original non-combustion chamber boiler fitted with a dome. No 6200 followed suit in June 1936. Three of these boilers had been built, but one was not fitted with a dome until about 1952. As boilers were changed at general repairs, therefore, both these two appeared with domeless boilers from time to time. The later boilers with combustion chambers could not be fitted to Nos 6200/01 until frame modifications had been made (see below).

5 In 1936 all the 'Princesses' were provided with new tenders with the top bunker side rollover extended to hold 10 ton of coal. One of these, attached to No 6206, was fitted with a steam-operated coal pusher, as a guinea pig for the 'Duchess' tenders which appeared a year later. This tender could be distinguished by the casing and pipes behind the rear bulkhead.

6 About 1937, in advance of the general removal, the dry trickle sanding was replaced by steam sanding on all 12 'Princesses'.

7 From 1938 the vacuum pumps were removed. This made it necessary to fit large and small ejectors, in a larger housing, in Nos 6200/01.

8 In 1938 a major modification was made to No 6205. The two inside sets of Walschaerts valve gear were removed and the inside valves driven by rocker arms in front of the outside cylinders from the outside gear. The most noticeable element of this modification was the massive new outside motion plate, in triangular form and bridging the leading coupled wheels; it was an inelegant solution. The reversing gear was altered at the same time; a new intermediate reversing shaft was inserted between intermediate and trailing coupled wheels below the platform and connected to the cab by a straight reach rod with platform-mounted steady bracket. There was a short linking rod to the existing reversing shaft.

9 Also in 1938 No 6212 was fitted with a modified smokebox door without the central dart fastening and with 10 securing dogs round the circumference.

10 In that year a start was made with fitting BTH speedometers, the generator of which was mounted on a bracket over the left trailing coupled wheel. Most if not all were fitted by the time the order was suspended in 1940. They quickly fell into disrepair and were removed.

Almost all modification work ceased during World War 2, but gradually as tubeplates needed to be renewed the superheaters on all boilers (except for the one with 40 elements, usually kept for No 6202) were standardised at 32 elements.

11 In 1952 the frames of Nos 6200/01 were modified to accept the later boilers with combustion chambers.

Below:
No 6201 *Princess Elizabeth* (Crewe, 11/35) when new, fitted with an experimental double stove pipe chimney, and plain bearing tender axleboxes. LMSR lined crimson lake livery.
National Railway Museum

Right:
Cylinders and motion of No 6201 in preservation, showing open-jawed slidebars with tiebar, open-fronted motion plate behind the leading coupled wheels with integral expansion link trunnions, eccentric rod attached to outside of link, anti-vacuum valve on outside main steampipe, steam operated cylinder cocks without discharge pipes, and an atomiser steam supply taken direct from the cylinder cock supply. *J. H. Cooper-Smith*

Curiously, after this neither of them ever again carried a non-combustion chamber boiler!

12 At this time, over a period of four years to 1956, all the domeless boilers were provided with domes. When this was done the regulator lubrication cock on the smokebox side was done away with.

13 Commencing in 1956 all 'Princesses' were fitted with steam-operated cylinder cocks; the usual manually-operated cocks, with their complex linkage, proved difficult to work reliably. With the new cocks the normal group of three discharge pipes forward from below each cylinder disappeared. With this modification

Below:
No 6203 *Princess Margaret Rose* (Crewe, 7/35) at Crewe North shed in 1938. It is seen here with a domeless combustion chamber boiler, the second style of chimney, hollow axles, altered motion plate with expansion link trunion brackets bolted on, expansion link with bottom tail, ball bearing end on eccentric rod, reversing reach rods with cross-shaft in front of trailing splasher, two ejectors and the vacuum pump still fitted. It is coupled to a Stanier 9-ton, 4,000gal tender. LMSR lined crimson lake livery. *Photomatic*

Left:
No 6203 at Derby, preserved, after return from Butlins Holiday Camp, Pwllheli in 1975. Combustion chamber boiler now fitted with dome, BR AWS and Smith-Stone speedometer. LMSR lined crimson lake livery (not strictly correct for No 6203 in this condition).
Ian Allan library

Below left:
No 46205 *Princess Victoria* (Crewe, 7/35) passing Stafford on a Euston-Carlisle express on 19 July 1958 with a combustion chamber boiler, altered motion plate, valve rocker in front of outside cylinder, altered reversing reach rod, still fitted with manually-operated cylinder cocks, and external tender sieve boxes. BR lined green livery with 1949 crest, power class 8P.   *J. B. Bucknall*

smaller passenger and mixed traffic locomotives. From 1950 a light/medium blue livery with black and white lining was applied to Nos 46206/8/10, but was judged unsatisfactory and the already adopted dark Brunswick green lined orange and black was standardised for them, with tender crest and the power class immediately below the number. Finally, in a flurry of regionalisation in 1958 four 'Princesses' were repainted in LMSR crimson lake, Nos 46200/4/7/8; the first and third had black edging lined yellow as in LMSR days, but there is some doubt about the lining of the other two.

Withdrawal

After spending periods in store and being reactivated for summer workings, Nos 46204/10/1/2 were withdrawn in October 1961, followed by No 46205 in the following month. The last to be condemned were Nos 46200/06 in November 1962.

Preserved Locomotives

Two 'Princesses' have survived, both carrying boilers with combustion chambers:
6201 *Princess Elizabeth*
    LMSR lined crimson lake livery
6203 *Princess Margaret Rose*
    LMSR lined crimson lake livery
    with 1957 BR crest.

the atomiser steam cock on the smokebox was also removed.
14 About 1957 the fitting started of Smith-Stone speedometers, with the generator mounted on a return crank on the left trailing crankpin.

Power Classification

The LMSR classified the 'Princesses' as 7P. This remained the case until 1951, when under the new BR system they became 8P.

Livery

Before World War 2 all were finished in LMSR crimson lake, edged black and lined yellow. So far as is known the only ones to be given the 1936 sans serif characters before these were abandoned in 1937 were Nos 6204/6/10/2. During the war the crimson lake gave way to unlined black, but as late as 1944 all were still in crimson lake, albeit very careworn. Six appear to have been turned out in

the 1946 LMSR livery of black with broad maroon stripes and edging lined in straw, namely Nos 6200/1/3/6/10/1.

With the advent of BR, six 'Princesses' (Nos 6201/5/7/9/11/2) appeared in black with red, grey and cream lining as later standardised for

LMSR Nos 6200/1/3-12

Orders and Construction

Nos	Builder	Lot No	Order No	Building Dates
6200, 6201	Crewe	99	E371	07/33, 11/33
6203-6212	Crewe	120	E395	07/35-10/35

Principal Dimensions

4 Cylinders: 16¼in dia × 28in stroke
Coupled Wheels: 6ft 6in
Boiler Pressure: 250lb/sq in
Grate Area: 45.0sq ft
Tractive Effort: 40,300lb

BR Nos 46200/1/3-12

Weight in Working Order:
    Locomotive: 104.5 ton
    Tender: 54.1 ton (original),
        56.35 ton (later)
    Total: 158.6 ton to 160.85 ton
Coal Capacity: 9 ton (original) 10 ton
        (later)
Water Capacity: 4,000gal

Class 7P - Turbine-Driven 4-6-2

History

The original intention for the 1933 Building Programme was that three conventional 'Princesses' should be built. In 1932, however, Stanier was persuaded by Metropolitan-Vickers Electrical Co (now a part of GEC-Alsthom) to visit Sweden to see a new 2-8-0 in operation powered by a Ljungstrom non-condensing steam turbine. This simple locomotive offered prospects of useful fuel economy. Stanier thus got sanction for the third 4-6-2 to be similarly powered, while otherwise broadly conforming to the 'Princess' design, even though it represented a 67% increase in first cost. No 6202 ran in this form for some 15 years, and inevitably was known (unofficially) as 'Turbomotive'. It encountered many teething troubles and was frequently in Crewe works for repairs, some of which were protracted. When a major failure occurred in 1950 it was accepted that nothing useful would be learned by prolonging the experiment and that no further steam turbine-driven locomotives would be built. The decision was therefore taken to rebuild No 46202 as a conventional four-cylinder locomotive, a hybrid between a 'Princess' and 'Duchess'.

Appearing as No 46202 *Princess Anne* in August 1952 it had little chance to demonstrate its capabilities before it was wrecked in the Harrow & Wealdstone multiple collision on 8 October 1952 and written off.

Features

No 6202 was generally similar in appearance to the second batch of 10 'Princesses', Nos 6203-6212. A boiler with combustion chamber was fitted, having no dome; internally this was identical with those put on Nos 6207-6212 new, having a 32-element superheater.

It was coupled to a Stanier 9-ton, 4,000gal tender.

There were, however, very significant differences:

1 The place of the cylinders was taken by rounded casings over the turbines, the forward turbine on the left-hand side and the smaller reverse turbine on the right.

2 Only coupling rods were provided; both turbines drove the leading coupled axle through trains of gears between the frames.

3 The frames at the front end were deeper; between them was a top-hinged door under the smokebox front which was open when running to admit cooling air for the lubricating oil radiators.

4 There was a deep full-length casing above the left-hand platform and a short one alongside the smokebox above the right-hand platform, containing the turbine steam valves and operating gear.

5 A double chimney was fitted.

Allocation

After a few months of preliminary testing, No 6202 was allocated to Camden shed. Except for occasional test turns it spent its working life taking a morning express from Euston to Liverpool, returning with the 17.25 'flyer'.

Below:
No 6202 (Crewe, 6/35) as-built, left-hand side. This shows the original domeless combustion chamber boiler, dry trickle sanding, roller bearings on all axles and double chimney. Stanier 4,000gal, 9-ton riveted tender. LMSR lined crimson lake livery. *Ian Allan library*

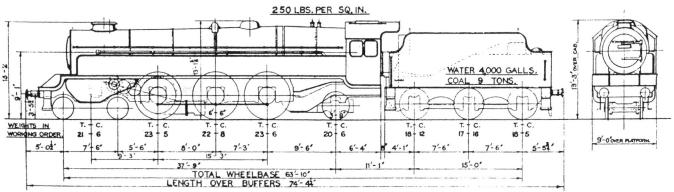

Class 7P 4-6-2, turbine driven, No 6202.

Modifications

1 In 1936, in the course of a works repair, a new boiler was fitted containing a larger (40-element) superheater and with a dome. At the same time the original dry trickle sanding was replaced by steam sanding equipment.
2 Late in 1939, smoke deflectors were fitted alongside the smokebox to overcome the exhaust beating down under the very soft blast conditions; they were straight with the tops angled inwards slightly, very similar to those applied to the parallel-boilered 'Royal Scots' about 1935.
3 In 1942 the locomotive emerged from Crewe with the right-hand side casing extended back nearly to the intermediate splasher, to house an additional lubricating oil pump.

Rebuilding

When No 46202 came from Crewe works in rebuilt form in August 1952 it was still very much a 'Princess', although perhaps improved in appearance and with significant changes to overcome weaknesses and move towards some of the improvements built into the 'Duchesses'.

A new front end was grafted on to the original frames, which reduced the coupled wheelbase from 8ft 0in+7ft 3in to two equal 7ft 3in spacings. The general layout of cylinders and Walschaerts valve gear was on 'Duchess' lines, with the outside cylinders between the bogie wheels. Outside valve gear only was used, the inside valves being driven by rocking levers behind the cylinders. The eccentric rods had ball bearing ends to the return cranks, with brass covers.

The side platforms were continuous in front of the cylinders, surprisingly, and raised several inches over the cylinders and valve gear, stepping down behind the intermediate coupled wheels. Very small splashers were provided. There was a substantial

casing over the outside steam pipes to outside and inside cylinders.

The existing boiler with combustion chamber, dome and 40-element superheater was reused, but a normal 'Princess' single chimney was fitted.

Power Classification

In LMSR parlance No 6202 was classed 7P, the same as the other Pacifics. When rebuilt the new BR classification was in force, making the locomotive 8P.

Livery

Until World War 2 No 6202 was turned out in normal LMSR crimson lake edged black and lined yellow. In 1944 it appeared in wartime unlined black, but in 1947 it appeared in the 1946 LMSR black livery with broad maroon bands lined straw. After rebuilding it was painted in standard BR dark green, lined out in orange and black with the current crest.

Withdrawal

The official date of withdrawal was May 1954, but for all practical purposes No 46202 was taken out of service in October 1952, following the Harrow accident.

LMSR No 6202   **BR No 46202**

Order and Production

Nos	Builder	Lot No	Order No	Built	Rebuilt
6202	Crewe	100	E371 (Part)	06/35	08/52

Principal Dimensions

	Original	Rebuilt
4 Cylinders:	—	16½in dia × 28in stroke
Coupled Wheels:	6ft 6in	6ft 6in
Boiler Pressure:	250lb/sq in	250lb/sq in
Grate Area:	45.0sq ft	45.0sq ft
Tractive Effort:	—	41,536lb
Weight in Working Order:		
Locomotive:	110.55 ton	Not published
Tender:	54.65 ton	54.65 ton
Total;	165.2 ton	Not published
Coal Capacity:	9 ton	9 ton
Water Capacity:	4,000gal	4,000gal

Class 7P - Four-Cylinder 4-6-2 'Coronation'/'Duchess'

History

In the 1930s the railways experienced growing competition, not only from road transport (internal air services were then in their infancy) but in some fields amongst themselves. The main Anglo-Scottish routes were a case in point. With the collapse of the 8¼hr agreement between the West Coast (LMSR) and East Coast (LNER) routes for London-Glasgow/Edinburgh trains, acceleration of services began in earnest. By 1935 the LNER had introduced a 4hr streamlined service between King's Cross and Newcastle,

Below:
Typical duty (1): No 6224 Princess Alexandra (Crewe, 7/37) on the down 'Coronation Scot' in 1937. The locomotive and train are in the special blue livery with silver horizontal stripes. *Ian Allan library*

the 'Silver Jubilee'; their public image was on the ascendant, and the LMSR needed to respond. In 1936 the LNER ran tests to confirm the feasibility of a 6hr King's Cross-Edinburgh timing, and planned to introduce such a service, the 'Coronation', in 1937. The LMSR ran a high-speed test between Euston and Glasgow in November 1936 with No 6201 *Princess Elizabeth,* which was very successful but showed that a 6hr timing was impracticable over this slightly longer and more difficult route. Even with a 6½hr timing and the load of nine coaches demanded by the commercial managers it was clear that some refinement of the 'Princess' design would be beneficial. This work was undertaken for Stanier by Tom Coleman, the chief draughtsman, and resulted in the

splendid streamlined four-cylinder 'Coronation' or 'Duchess' class.

They were to prove not only very fast, holding for a year the British speed record at 114mph set on 29 June 1937, but also capable of tremendous load haulage. Postwar tests at the Rugby Testing Station were unable to push them to the limit of their power.

Features

As compared with the 'Princesses' the coupled wheels were increased in diameter by three inches and the coupled wheelbase reduced to 14ft 6in. The outside cylinders were moved forward to the more usual position between the bogie wheels. Unlike Stanier's other designs, the valve spindle crosshead guides were

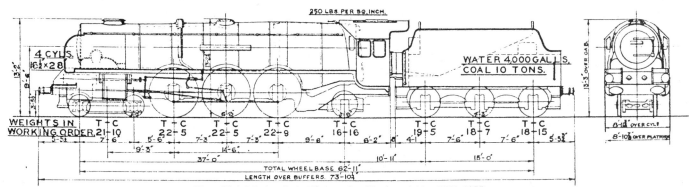

Class 7P 4-6-2, 4-cylinder 'Coronation/Duchess', Nos 6220-6255

mounted on the motion plate, clear of the cylinders; this provided space for the linkage to the rocking levers driving the inside valves from the outside motion. The eccentric rod featured a ball bearing end at the return crank, while the crosshead arm was secured behind rather than below the crosshead gudgeon pin and inclined towards the rear, a very uncommon arrangement. A Stone-Deuta speedometer was fitted, with the generator mounted on a bracket over the left trailing coupled wheel and a horizontal conduit from it for the cable to the cab. The rear end of the frames below the firebox used the same splayed sandwich construction as on the 'Princesses'.

A maximum size boiler with wide Belpaire firebox incorporating a combustion chamber was fitted. The fire-

Above:
**No 6232 *Duchess of Montrose* (Crewe, 7/38)
when new.** At this date it has a single chimney,
vacuum ejectors in forward position,
continuous platform in front of the cylinders,
reversing reach rod under the running plate,
BTH speedometer, vee-fronted cab with large
front windows, 10-ton, 4,000gal welded tender
cut down front and rear to cab door level, with
D openings in the frames. Photographic grey
simulation of LMSR crimson lake livery with
gold lining. *Ian Allan library*

box was wider than that of the
'Princesses', to give a larger grate area
within the same length. The entire
boiler, smokebox, cylinders and front
end were covered in a streamlined
casing with rounded, curved front
from which the chimney barely protruded. Though this casing swelled
out at platform level, there was no flat
walkway. It was cut away over the
coupled wheels and motion, and
bulged slightly over the cylinders, and
below them to cover the bypass valves.
Washout inspection doors on the
firebox shoulders, washout plugs at
crown level, sandbox fillers, etc were
inset in this casing and a straight
nameplate was attached. There were
various flush access doors and panels
for mechanical lubricators, vacuum
ejectors, etc. Access to the smokebox
was via a pair of side-hinged front
doors, with a single open step below
the inset drawhook and steps and door
and grab handles above. Only these
and a full-length handrail broke the
smooth outline.

The cab was of the usual double
side-window type, but was vee-
fronted, with relatively narrow front
windows; rubber sheeting covered the
gap between the cab roof and the
tender front bulkhead.

The tender was a modification of the
4,000gal 10-ton tender by now running behind the 'Princesses', and of
welded construction. The side sheets

Above:
**No 6234 *Duchess of Abercorn* (Crewe, 8/38)
when nearly new,** with hopper ashpan
operating gear on the rear frames. LMSR
crimson lake livery with gold lining.
Real Photographs

Right:
**No 6252 *City of Leicester* (Crewe, 6/44) when
new.** It has a double chimney, continuous
running plate in front of the cylinders, BTH
speedometer. It is coupled to a streamlined
tender with high cut-out at cab, high back,
valance and covered D frame openings. LMSR
plain wartime black livery. *Ian Allan library*

at the cab opening were taken up a
little higher, and at the rear end were
continued at full height into a fairing
which projected beyond the rear of the
tank; a sliding door each side gave
access to the two tank filler holes. A
side valance was provided below the
tank bottom, and the D-shaped frame
lightening holes were fitted with cover
plates. The bunker contained a steam-
operated coal pusher, with the control
mechanism etc housed under a casing
behind the rear bunker bulkhead; it
exhausted into the tank.

Allocation

The first five of the class were divided
between Camden and Polmadie depots

for working the 'Coronation Scot' trains. As more were built they took up residence at these depots, together with Crewe North, and Carlisle Upperby. Though they also worked into Liverpool they were never allocated to Edge Hill shed in that city.

Changes in Production

1 Only No 6220 (6/37) was built with the single footstep below the front drawhook. All subsequent examples had a second footstep added; the whole arrangement looked rather flimsy but proved adequate. It may be that No 6220 was also modified before going into traffic.

2 Starting with No 6225 (Crewe, 5/38) a change was made to the brake hangers, to take two articulated brake blocks on each; this was done to reduce block wear in high-speed braking. This was standardised for all future builds, but was not applied retrospectively to Nos 6220-6224.

3 Also from No 6225 a small ventilation grille was provided in the streamlined casing in front of the outside cylinders. The bypass valves were also omitted, and so the flare at the bottom of the casing to clear them disappeared.

4 Further changes introduced from No 6225 were the provision of a cowl about 3ft 9in long over the front of the tender bunker, and the substitution of BTH speedometers for the previous Stone-Deuta type.

5 No 6229 (Crewe, 9/38) was fitted with a drop grate and hopper ashpan; the operating gear for the hopper doors protruded through the rear end frames on the right-hand side, immediately behind the two oval lightening slots.

6 The next five, Nos 6230 (Crewe, 7/38) to 6234 were built without streamlining, revealing further changes from the 'Princesses' which had previously been hidden. On the boiler the dome and top-feed were moved further forward than in previous practice, and a shapely single chimney was fitted in place of the previous stovepipe under the streamlining. The vacuum ejectors were moved forward to the front of the boiler barrel, set low and with only a short exhaust pipe. There were conventional front and side platforms joined by curved drop sections in front of the cylinders. On each platform over the intermediate coupled wheels were two mechanical lubricators. A sizeable casing enclosed the main steam pipes which branched outside the smokebox to inside and outside cylinders.

The vee-fronted cab was retained, but with no streamlined casing the opportunity was taken to enlarge the front windows. There was no rubber sheeting from roof to tender.

7 No 6234 (Crewe, 8/38) was fitted with a drop grate and hopper ashpan similar to those on No 6229.

8 The tenders for these five non-streamlined locomotives were also modified. The front cab opening was cut away lower to the level of the cab doors, at the back end there was no extended fairing and the sides were cut down similarly to those on the 'Princesses' for easier water column access. The bottom valance was also omitted, and the D-shaped frame lightening holes were left open.

9 Beginning with No 6235 (Crewe, 7/39) streamlining was resumed. The drop grate and hopper ashpan used on Nos 6229 (by now renumbered 6220) and 6234 was adopted for the future. A double blastpipe and chimney were fitted from new, following the successful outcome of the tests with No 6234 in February 1939; this feature was not easy to identify on the streamlined locomotives.

10 Commencing with No 6249 (Crewe, 4/44) streamlining was abandoned, and locomotives carried the continuous front/side platforms with valance angles as on No 6230. However, four tenders had already been built in streamlined form with extended sides, bottom valances and covered frame slots, and these were attached to Nos 6249-6252.

11 The next three, Nos 6253 (Crewe, 9/46) – 6255, exhibited further developments. The side and front platforms were of lightweight construction with shallower folded edges instead of an angle valance, and were discontinuous in front of the cylinders to facilitate withdrawal of the piston valves. Smoke deflectors were fitted alongside the smokebox, angled inwards from just above the platform; they contained two inset handgrips and at the front finished at the level of the bottom of the platform edge. A rocking grate and a hopper ashpan of new design were provided; the operating gear for the hopper doors was

below the cab floor and thus out of sight. Blow-off cocks were fitted on the right-hand side of the firebox near the front, with vertical discharge pipe. The locomotives had self-cleaning smokeboxes, evident from the 'SC' plates below the shed plates.

12 The tenders for Nos 6253-6255 were no longer all-welded; the internal baffle plates were attached by riveting. The front cutaway at the cab remained high, as on the streamlined tenders, while the back end was similar to those on Nos 6230-6234. The D-shaped frame lightening holes were left open, but those between leading and intermediate wheels were partially obscured by external sieve boxes for the injector feeds. Modified tender spring links pinned directly to the frame brackets were used.

13 The final two 'Duchesses', Nos 6256 (Crewe, 12/47) and 46257 brought further changes, mainly in the area below the firebox. The prominent splayed rear section frames were replaced by simple bar frame extensions and the hitherto standard plate frame trailing truck by a one-piece cast steel truck, identifiable by the flanges on the radial arms and the three triangular lightening holes each side. There was immediate trouble with cracking of this truck on No 6256 and the release of No 46257 to traffic was delayed while a new design of fabricated one-piece truck was produced. This later truck was distinguishable by the square box-section radial arms and single circular lightening hole each side. A new type of hopper ashpan, with no external operating gear visible, had shallow hinged side doors the full length of the firebox for raking purposes. Blow-off cocks were fitted on the right-hand side of the firebox as on Nos 6253-6255. Roller bearing axle-boxes (Timken) were provided throughout; the outside axleboxes on the trailing truck and tender revealed this by the circular cover plates, later painted yellow.

The cab sides were cut off square at floor level, about 14in below the side platforms, leaving much daylight below them. An inclined tubular reversing shaft from the cab was coupled to the actual reversing screw below the platform between intermediate and trailing coupled wheels, with a short reach rod to the reversing shaft. The tender was again modified, bringing the cab opening down to cab door height, giving a similar profile to those on Nos 6230-6234.

During their enforced wait for the new trailing trucks the two were fitted with electric lighting, the Stone turbo-generator being carried on a bracket low down on the right-hand side of the smokebox to the rear of the smoke

deflector. They were also fitted with an early form of Smith-Stone speedometer, the generator being carried on a return crank on the left trailing crankpin.

14 At some stage, probably from No 6235 the tender coal pusher was rearranged to exhaust to atmosphere. The short vertical pipes came from the control casing to the top of the tender bulkhead. This resulted in operation of the pusher being revealed by alternating plumes of steam at the back of the bunker.

Modifications

1 No 6234 was fitted with a double blastpipe and chimney in the course of fast 600-ton trials between Crewe and Glasgow in 2/39. As a result of the higher power sustainable with this double exhaust the remaining ex-

amples with single chimneys were similarly equipped, the first being No 6224 (5/40) and the last No 6220 (12/44).

2 To prevent drifting steam from obscuring the view of drivers on non-streamlined versions, which may have contributed to one or two accidents where signals were overrun, smoke deflectors were fitted retrospectively. The first to be dealt with was No 6232 (2/45) and the last No 6249 (11/46). Those locomotives, with continuous platforms, had the deflectors taken down to front platform level, the bottom section being slightly inset and fitted with a vertical grab handle.

3 Removal of streamlining began with No 6235 in April 1946; in some cases locomotives ran in this form for less than four years. This gave the class two new features. The side platforms, of the lightweight folded and discontinuous type, were similar

to those on Nos 6253-6257. Smoke deflectors were fitted, finishing at upper platform level; the grab handle in these cases was fitted horizontally on the front platform. This work continued until May 1949, when the last to be converted, No 46243 was de-streamlined. The other feature was that the original smokeboxes were seen as chamfered off on top in front of the chimney, though the smokebox door was circular. As smokebox renewals became necessary, normal circular smokeboxes were fitted, No 46235 being the first dealt with

(7/52) and No 46246 the last (5/60). On the tenders, de-streamlining led to removal of the side valances and the removal of lightening hole covers. The side sheets were cut down at the rear end to conform to those on Nos 6230-6234. In a few cases the front cab opening was also cut down to cab door height, but the majority were not altered in this respect.

4 In 1950 No 46256 acquired an axle-driven generator on the left-hand end of the leading bogie axle; it was coupled to the Smith-Stone speedometer to give steadier indications at low speeds. It only lasted about a year before removal.

5 A curious reversion took place on No 46242 when rebuilt after the major damage sustained in the Harrow & Wealdstone collision in 1952. After having been given discontinuous platforms when de-streamlined in March 1947, it reappeared after repair with continuous platforms and smoke deflectors down to front platform level!

6 In the early 1950s the narrow cab front windows of the formerly streamlined locomotives were progressively replaced by larger windows as on the non-streamlined examples.

7 At about this time also the fitting of external sieve boxes to the tenders of Nos 6220-6252 was undertaken.

8 Contemporary with this was the application of mileage recorders to the tenders of Nos 46256/57. They were mounted on the left leading axlebox cover, but were removed after a few years.

9 In the late 1950s a start was made on fitting Smith-Stone speedometers. The generator was mounted as usual on a return crank on the left trailing crankpin.

10 At about this time the boiler blow-off cocks were removed from Nos 46253-46257.

Power Classification

Classed 7P by the LMSR, the 1951 BR classification scheme altered the 'Duchesses' to 8P without in any way affecting their permitted loads.

Livery

The first five locomotives, Nos 6220-6224, were turned out in Coronation blue with four silver horizontal stripes, two broad flanking two narrower, within which the sans serif number and 'LMS' were set. The stripes came down to a point above the bottom centre lamp bracket. All but one (No 6221) retained this livery until succumbing to wartime unlined black in 1944.

The second five (Nos 6225-6229) came out in identical style but in LMSR crimson lake with gold stripes, and after the five non-streamlined examples, the next 10 streamlined ones (Nos 6235-6244) were painted likewise. They, too, became unlined black in 1944/45. Nos 6230-6234 came out in standard crimson lake, but the usual yellow lining was executed in gold and very thinly edged in vermilion. This painting lasted particularly well, only No 6231 getting plain black. Nos 6245-6248 were painted unrelieved black from new.

Practically all 'Duchesses' received the 1946 livery of black with maroon bands edged straw and with sans serif characters; there was some variation in the lining (or not) of certain boiler bands. The exceptions were No 6243,

Left:
No 46250 *City of Lichfield* **(Crewe, 5/44) at Euston about 1958, with continuous front running plate, hopper ashpan operating gear on the rear frames, and external tender sieve boxes. BR lined green livery with 1957 crest.**
BR LM Region

son lake. Initially the lining was inset from panel edges in yellow and black, but later this gave way to lining in the LMSR style, while using the 1957 crest on the tender. These two schemes, either GWR dark green or LMSR crimson lake, lasted until withdrawal. From September 1964 a broad yellow diagonal stripe was painted on each cab panel to indicate that they were not permitted to work under the 25kV overhead wires south of Crewe.

Withdrawal

The first three examples were withdrawn in December 1962 (Nos 46227/31/2). 13 were taken out of service in 1963, and the remainder in 1964, the last in service being No 46256 which was withdrawn in 10/64.

Preserved Locomotives

Three 'Duchesses' have been preserved:

46229 *Duchess of Hamilton*
at the National Railway Museum, York, in BR/LMSR crimson lake with 1957 BR crest.

6233 *Duchess of Sutherland*
at Bressingham, in LMSR crimson lake, edged black with yellow lining.

46235 *City of Birmingham*
at Birmingham Museum of Science & Industry, in BR dark green, lined orange and black with 1957 BR crest.

which went from unlined black to BR blue, and No 6234, which in early 1946 was painted in a blue-grey as a prototype for the postwar livery, but this was not adopted.

Under British Railways there was considerable vacillation over liveries for the first 18 months. Six of the class were painted a darkish blue with LNWR lining of red, grey and cream during 1948, together with No 46244 in a paler shade of blue with black and yellow lining. Between October 1948 and May 1949 seven were painted black with LNWR red, grey and cream lining; both these schemes used 'British Railways' in full and the lined tender panel extended up only to the bend in the side.

In 1949 BR adopted a livery of light blue, lined in black and edged white, for the class. The first to be so treated was No 46244 (1/49) and bore the BR crest. 25 more were similarly painted between 5/49 and 10/51, by which time it had been decided that the best colour scheme for principal passenger classes was GWR Brunswick green with orange and black lining. All except one 'Duchess', No 46240,

received this livery, the first being No 46232 in November 1951. The later tender crest was adopted in 1957.

1958 saw another change, with 16 of the class repainted in LMSR crim-

LMSR Nos 6220-6256

BR Nos 46220-46257*

*Construction continued by British Railways

Orders and Construction

Nos	Builder	Lot No	Order No	Building Dates
6220-6224	Crewe	138	E402	06/37-07/37
6225-6234	Crewe	145	E408	05/38-09/38
6235-6244	Crewe	150	E414	07/39-07/40
6245-6252	Crewe	150	E415	06/43-06/44
6253-6255	Crewe	184	E464	09/46-10/46
6256, 46257	Crewe	184	E464	12/47, 05/48

Principal Dimensions

4 Cylinders: 16½in dia × 28in stroke
Coupled Wheels: 6ft 9in
Boiler Pressure: 250lb/sq in
Weight in Working Order:

Grate Area: 50.0sq ft
Tractive Effort: 40,000lb

	Streamlined	Non-streamlined
Locomotive:	108.1 ton	105.25 ton†
Tender:	56.35 ton	56.35 ton†
Total:	164.45 ton	161.6 ton†

Coal Capacity: 10 ton
Water Capacity: 4,000gal
†Nos 46256/57, 108.5/56.5/165.0 ton

Class 8F - 2-8-0

History

The LMSR's need for a good, versatile heavy freight locomotive was serious when Stanier became CME in 1932. The only major locomotives the railway had produced had been the 33 Beyer-Garratts for mineral haulage on the Midland Division and 175 Class 7F 0-8-0s mainly for use on the Western and Central Divisions, which were completed by mid-1932. Both classes had serious maintenance problems resulting from their Midland ancestry, and were not suitable to deal with the gradual acceleration of goods trains which was taking place. The arrival of the new Class 7F (soon to be uprated to 8F) 2-8-0s filled a gaping void in the fleet with great distinction.

With the onset of World War 2 the design was chosen as a War Department standard for overseas use, and orders were placed for 240 locomotives with three builders, while another 51 were requisitioned from LMSR stock. But with the fall of France in 1940 there was only one theatre of war to which they could be sent, namely the Middle East, needing relatively modest numbers. The initial orders were curtailed to 100 locomotives, but further deliveries took place in 1941/42 to a total of 208. During and after hostilities some 73 '8Fs' built for or requisitioned by the Government were handed over to the LMSR or BR – the last three as late as 1957. The design was also adopted by the wartime Railway Executive Committee as a standard for use on the LNER, GWR and SR rather than build other company types, and they were built in six works belonging to those railways.

In all 852 Class 8F 2-8-0s were built to this design, and at its peak in 1957 the BR stock of them was 666.

Features

The chassis, cylinders and motion showed many of the features of the contemporary Class 5 4-6-0s, and many components were standard with them: cylinders, much of the motion details, axleboxes, etc. They had an almost identical Walschaerts long-travel valve gear, with the Horwich-style crosshead arm with two bolt fastening and straight fluted combination lever. The coupled wheel balance weights were of built-up type, the plates finishing square at a spoke. Both mechanical lubricators were on the right-hand platform. All axles were bored hollow.

The boiler, with straight throatplate and no dome (Class 3C) was similar to that of the early Class 5s but was approximately 12in shorter in the barrel. The front of the firebox sat over the driving axleboxes, so that the transition between boiler barrel and firebox was directly over the axle centre. The superheater was of 21 elements, and there were two washout inspection doors with domed covers on the firebox shoulders and five washout plugs at crown level on each side. The top-feed delivery pipes were set flush into the boiler clothing.

The usual double side-window cab was fitted, and the reversing reach rod from it was curved down at the front end with a tall steady bracket from the side platform halfway along it. Steam brakes only were provided, with no ability to work vacuum-fitted trains. The locomotive was coupled to a standard 4,000gal 9-ton tender of riveted construction.

Allocation

The first examples were initially allocated to Willesden, Toton (Nottingham) and Wellingborough. As numbers increased they were sent to

Class 8F 2-8-0, 2-cylinder, Nos 8012-8125

Left:

Left:
Not so typical duty: No 48631 (Brighton, 6/43) climbing the 1 in 105 approaching Marsden with a Leeds-Belle Vue excursion on 23 April 1962. *N. A. Machell*

Above:
No 8000 (Crewe, 6/35) as-built, with a domeless straight throatplate boiler, washout inspection doors on the firebox shoulders, Horwich-type crosshead arm, built-up balance weights, curved reversing reach rod with tall steady-bracket, dry trickle sanding, no vacuum brake, hollow coupled axles, and a riveted 4,000gal tender. *Ian Allan library*

depots the length and breadth of the country, though the concentration of Class 7F 0-8-0s (in due course superseded by WD 2-8-0s) on the Central Division ensured that very few sheds there had them. After working in Scotland during World War 2 (including some sterling work on passenger trains) they were all displaced to English sheds as WD 2-8-0s were purchased. The biggest allocations were to Toton, Willesden, Wellingborough, Kirkby and Westhouses.

Changes during Production

1 Commencing with No 8006 (Crewe, 9/35) vacuum brake equipment was fitted. The single ejector was mounted in front of the cab with long exhaust pipe to the smokebox. These single ejectors were identifiable by the smaller body with a horizontal steam passage cast along the outside, and the single steam pipe from the cab.
2 Beginning with No 8027 (Vulcan, 7/36) and No 8012 (Crewe, 12/36) a revised boiler design with sloping

throatplate was adopted as standard. The boiler barrel/firebox transition moved forward as a result to a position about 12in in front of the driving axle. There were still five washout plugs on the left side of the firebox, but six on the right-hand side. A dome was provided behind the top-feed; the casing of the latter was of the usual slender form, with the feed pipes only partially 'submerged' in the boiler clothing. The atomiser steam cock was moved higher up on the smokebox. The Horwich-style crosshead arm was changed to a Derby-type arm with three-stud fastening to the crosshead and a union link forked at both ends. Steam sanding replaced the previous dry trickle sanding equipment.
3 From No 8096 (Crewe, 12/38) tenders of welded construction were fitted. Ball bearing eccentric rod ends were also introduced.
4 Beginning with No 8126 (Crewe, 1/41) the connecting rods were shortened from 11ft 3in to 10ft 10in centres to enable piston rings to be changed without 'breaking' the piston rod/crosshead joint. This was evident in the longer union links (15in instead of 10in) and the reduced length of chamfer at the rear end of the slidebars.
5 The locomotives built on War Department account in 1940-42 (and which subsequently became LMSR Nos 8246-8297 and BR Nos 48773/4 were built with 10ft 10in connecting rods similar to No 8126, and with the curved reversing reach rod and tall steady bracket. They had solid axles and were coupled to riveted tenders.
6 No 8146 (Crewe, 7/42) was the first

to be fitted with a new pattern straight reversing reach rod and shorter steady bracket.
7 From No 8156 (Crewe, 11/42) the use of ball bearing eccentric rod ends was discontinued and reversion made to plain bearings.
8 The use of hollow axles on LMSR-built locomotives ceased with No 8165 (Crewe, 3/43). Thereafter all Crewe and Horwich-built 2-8-0s and all those built at other railways works had solid axles.
9 Starting with No 8176 (NBL, 3/42) there was a reversion to tenders with riveted tanks. In addition two vacuum ejectors were provided, in a somewhat enlarged body.

Henceforward the situation became complicated thanks to simultaneous construction in LNER, GWR and SR works and the transfer of some WD-ordered locomotives into LMSR stock. In addition certain design changes were permitted to ease production under wartime conditions, to suit the equipment of individual works or to overcome material shortages.
10 Hitherto all Class 8Fs built on LMSR or WD account had had built-up balance weights in the coupled wheels, finishing square at a spoke. Evidently a decision was taken late in 1943 to allow crescent-shaped integral cast balance weights as an alternative; lead alloy for built-up balance weights was in very short supply. It is now very difficult to pinpoint the start of the use of integral cast balance weights, and the practice does not appear to have been clear-cut with particular orders but a little frayed at the edges, but it

Below:
**Typical duty (if not standard of cleanliness!):
No 48375 (Horwich, 11/44) leaving Astley Green
Colliery sidings on a special coal train on
12 May 1965.** *J. R. Carter*

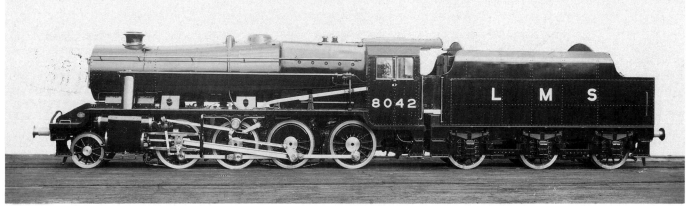

Top:
No 48003 (Crewe, 6/35) in the 1950s, fitted with a domed sloping throatplate boiler, steam sanding, and vacuum brake with single ejector. *Real Photographs*

Above:
No 8042 (VF, 9/36) as-built. It has a sloping throatplate boiler with dome, steam sanding, single vacuum ejector, Derby-style crosshead arm and union link, and a riveted tender. 1936 sans serif characters (unshaded).
BR LM Region

appears that the '8Fs' were built as shown, right:

11 Beginning with No 8301 (Crewe, 9/43) all '8Fs' built at Crewe, Horwich and Swindon were turned out with welded tenders. Those built at Darlington and Doncaster (Nos 8500-8559 and 8730-8772) were coupled to riveted tenders. All '8Fs' built in Southern workshops (Nos 8600-8729) emerged with welded tenders.

12 No 8490 (Horwich, 6/45) was built with a rocking grate and hopper ashpan, the only Class 8F so fitted, as an experiment. The hopper door operating gear in this case was immediately behind the trailing coupled

Builder	First No	Last No	Balance Weights
Crewe	all to 8322 (02/44)		Built up
	8323 (02/44)	8330 (05/44)	Integral cast
Horwich	8331 (09/43)	8337 (12/43)	Built up
	8338 (01/44)	8382 (01/45)	Integral cast
	8383 (01/45)	8399 (06/45)	Built up
	8490 (06/45)	8495 (08/45)	Built up
Swindon	8400 (06/43)	8429 (01/44)	Built up
	8430 (03/44)	8479 (07/45)	Integral cast
Darlington	8500 (02/44)	8509 (11/44)	Integral cast
	8540 (12/44)	8559 (08/45)	Built up
	8730 (09/45)	8752 (10/46)	Integral cast
Doncaster	8510 (06/43)	8539 (08/45)	Built up*
	8753 (10/45)	8772 (06/46)	Built up
Eastleigh	8600 (02/43)	8609 (10/43)	Built up
	8650 (10/43)	8662 (07/44)	Integral cast
Ashford	8610 (04/43)	8612 (07/43)	Built up
	8618 (09/43)	8624 (12/43)	Built up
	8671 (12/43)	8674 (03/44)	Not known
Brighton	8613 (07/43)	8617 (11/43)	Built up
	8625 (04/43)	8643 (11/43)	Built up
	8644 (11/43)	8649 (12/43)	Integral cast
	8663 (02/44)	8670 (07/44)	Integral cast
	8675 (03/44)	8704 (06/44)	Integral cast
	8705 (06/44)	9709 (06/44)	Built up
	8710 (07/44)	8729 (09/44)	Integral cast

*Some at least with snap head rivets.
However, this situation did not remain static; see 'Modifications'.

Top:
WD No 300 (NBL, 9/40) as-built. The locomotive has 10ft 10in connecting rods with longer slidebars and union link, built-up balance weights, solid axles, Westinghouse brake pump and reservoir, and coupling chains. This locomotive ran as LMSR No 8226 from new until September 1941. *BR LM Region*

Above:
No 48147 (Crewe, 7/42) at Willesden shed on 31 August 1949. It has 10ft 10in connecting rods, straight reversing reach rod with short steady bracket, solid axles, and eccentric rod with non-standard ball bearing end. No crest or inscription on tender. *H. C. Casserley*

wheels on the left-hand side, below the cab.

13 All six members of the Horwich batch Nos 8490-8495 were fitted with self-cleaning smokeboxes under experimental procedure; so far as is known there was no external indication.

14 Brighton-built Nos 8710 (7/44) to 8729 for the LNER (originally carrying LNER Nos 7651-7675, subsequently renumbered 3100-3124 and again in 1947 to 3500-3524 before transfer to the LMSR) were built with

Wakefield mechanical lubricators instead of the standard Silvertown pattern. They were of somewhat different shape and had external handwheels instead of double-ended handles.

Modifications

1 From about 1938 Nos 8000-8011 were fitted with steam sanding instead of the original dry trickle sanding equipment.

2 At about the same time (first general repair) Nos 8000-8005 were fitted with vacuum brakes, using a single ejector.

3 In May 1938 No 8003 received frame modifications to enable a sloping throatplate boiler to be fitted. This provided a spare straight throatplate boiler for exchange at general repairs. This was then the only one of the first 12 of the class to have a domed boiler.

4 In 1946 a scheme was started to fit 50 selected Class 8Fs at Toton and Wellingborough with blow-off cocks on the front of the firebox between the

frames as part of a controlled water softening experiment, and to confine them to the route between Toton and Brent. The locomotives so fitted could be identified by the blow-off cock operating rod along the right-hand side of the firebox just above the platform and the large 'X' painted on each cab side below the number. The experiment was terminated in the mid-1950s.

5 In late 1946 and 1947, 11 Class 8Fs were fitted for oil firing, with oil tanks fitted into the coal bunkers of the existing tenders. This was part of an extensive Government-sponsored scheme involving 1,217 locomotives, 245 of them Class 8Fs. It was called off due to cost and the improvement in coal supplies. No 8696 was the first to be converted, and was also the last to revert to coal firing, in April 1949.

6 From the 1950s there was some interchange of coupled wheels at works repairs; some '8Fs' built with integral cast balance weights acquired wheels with built-up balance weights and vice versa. Furthermore they were not always changed in complete sets; for instance Nos 48329 and 48402 ran with hybrid sets comprising three pairs of wheels with integral cast weights and the trailing wheels with built-up weights!

7 At some time in the 1950s No 48169 was fitted with a complete set of coupled wheels from a Riddles WD 2-8-0; the reason is not known, since it resulted in the locomotive having no reciprocating balance.

8 In 1955 two '8Fs', Nos 48309 and 48707 were fitted specially with steam heating equipment (hoses at the tender end only) to enable them to work a Royal Train over the Central

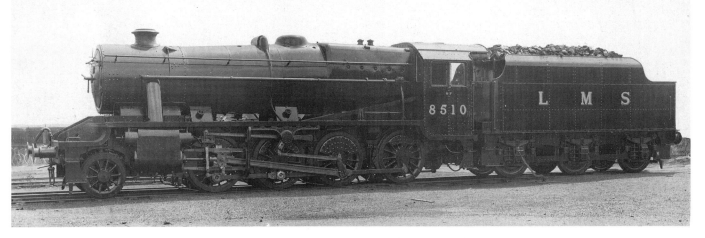

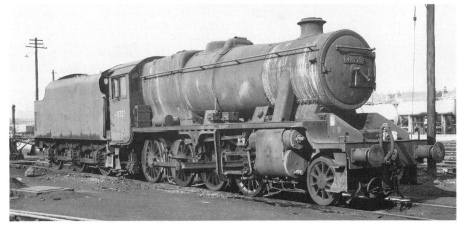

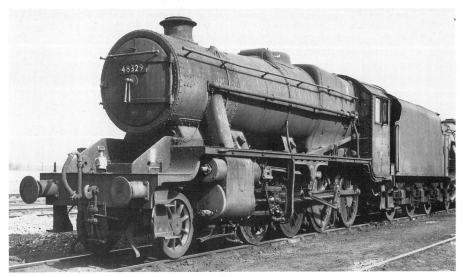

Top:
No 48177 (NBL, 3/42) in the 1950s, running with integral cast balance weights throughout; it was not built with them. *W. S. Sellar*

Above:
No 8510 (Doncaster, 6/43) when new, with large and small ejectors, built-up balance weights with snap head rivets, and disc wheels on the tender. *Ian Allan library*

Left:
No 48725 (Brighton, 9/44) on Gloucester shed in February 1966. Built as LNER No 7671, renumbered 3120 in 1946 and 3520 in 1947. It is fitted with Wakefield mechanical lubricators, 'top hat' on top-feed casing, BR AWS, top lamp bracket moved down, electrification flashes, integral cast balance weights, exhaust steam injector blanked off, and has a welded tender tank. *N. E. Preedy*

Below left:
No 48329 (Crewe, 4/44) on Banbury shed on 4 April 1965, running with integral cast balance weights on the leading, intermediate and driving axles, and built-up weights on the trailing axle, BR AWS, welded tender tank, and electrification flashes. *P. L. Simpson*

Wales line. The fittings were removed at next overhaul.

9 The last two '8Fs' purchased by BR from the War Department, Nos 48774/75 in July 1957 came with much enlarged top-feed casings from which shut-off cock spindles protruded. These two were never altered back to standard.

10 In the late 1950s a number of '8Fs' were transferred to the Western Region, all in the Swindon-built 484XX series; these had the LMSR-